Palmyra

Palmyra

An Irreplaceable Treasure

Originally published as
Palmyre: L'irremplaçable trésor

By

PAUL VEYNE

Translated from the French by
Teresa Lavender Fagan

The University of Chicago Press
Chicago and London

Publication of this book has been aided by a grant from the Neil Harris Endowment Fund, which honors the innovative Scholarship of Neil Harris, the Preston and Sterling Morton Professor Emeritus of History at the University of Chicago. The fund is supported by contributions from the students, colleagues, and friends of Neil Harris.

The University of Chicago Press, Chicago 60637
The University of Chicago Press, Ltd., London
© 2017 by The University of Chicago
Published 2017
Paperback edition 2018
Printed in the United States of America

Originally published as *Palmyre: L'irremplaçable trésor.* © Editions Albin Michel - Paris 2015

27 26 25 24 23 22 21 20 19   2 3 4 5

ISBN-13: 978-0-226-42782-9 (cloth)
ISBN-13: 978-0-226-60005-5 (paper)
ISBN-13: 978-0-226-45293-7 (e-book)
DOI: https://doi.org/10.7208/chicago/9780226452937.001.0001

Library of Congress Cataloging-in-Publication Data

Names: Veyne, Paul, 1930–author. | Fagan, Teresa Lavender, translator.
Title: Palmyra : an irreplaceable treasure / by Paul Veyne ; translated from the French by Teresa Lavender Fagan.
Other titles: Palmyre. English
Description: Chicago ; London : The University of Chicago Press, 2017. | Originally published as: Palmyre: l'irremplaçable trésor. | Includes bibliographical references.
Identifiers: LCCN 2016052000 | ISBN 9780226427829 (cloth : alk. paper) | ISBN 9780226452937 (e-book)
Subjects: LCSH: Tadmur (Syria)—History.
Classification: LCC DS99.P17 V4913 2017 | DDC 939.4/32—DC23
LC record available at https://lccn.loc.gov/2016052000

♾ This paper meets the requirements of ANSI/NISO Z39.48-1992 (Permanence of Paper).

To Khaled al-Assad,
archaeologist and head of antiquities for Palmyra from 1963 to 2003,
assassinated for "being the director of idolatry"

Contents

Translator's Note

As Paul Veyne says in the introduction to this wonderful little book, his intent is not to write a scholarly work on the ancient city of Palmyra. Rather, this book is a tribute to an unfathomably destroyed historical treasure. One can sense and share the author's grief, his passion for Palmyra, its monuments, its people, its art.

And as an impassioned tribute, the reader will find references to works without citations, perhaps passages that seem to arise straight from the author's heart, prose that is closer to the realm of poetry than that of scholarship. Wherever possible, I have provided additional information and footnotes to clarify a point, and have used published English translations of passages from texts in other languages.

As I write this note, Palmyra has been recaptured from ISIS, the group that was bent on her destruction. This is, of course, a very positive turn of events. And yet many of the ancient monuments and the irreplaceable art they contained, artifacts that brought the ancient city to life, are gone forever. And so we are all the more fortunate to have Paul Veyne's work on this extraordinary city, its people, and its unique place in history.

Introduction

Having studied Greco-Roman antiquity my entire profes-
sional life, I have often encountered Palmyra. Of course its
destruction by the terrorist organization Daesh (ISIS) did
not simply destroy the subject of my research; it obliterated
an entire fragment of our culture.

A dozen or so years ago, I wrote a long preface about Palmyra in a wonderful book of art and photography by Gérard
Degeorge.[1] In 2005 that text was expanded, enhanced with
scholarly notes, and republished in a book series I coedited
for Éditions du Seuil.[2]

This small book is completely different: it is much shorter,
and it is written not for scholars but for general readers. It
allows me to raise new questions, because current events are
pressing.

Why does a terrorist group destroy inoffensive monuments from the distant past (or put objects up for sale)? Why
did they destroy Palmyra, which was classified by UNESCO
as a World Heritage Site? And why are there so many massacres, including the torture, suffering, and decapitation, on
August 18, 2015, of the Palmyrene archeologist Khaled al-
Assaad, to whom I dedicate this book?

In spite of my advanced age, it is my duty as a former professor and as a human being to voice my stupefaction before this incomprehensible destruction, and to sketch a portrait of the past splendor of Palmyra, which now can only be known and experienced through books.

1

Riches in the Desert

A current victim of terrorist barbarism, the Greco-Roman archeological site of Palmyra was perhaps the most extraordinary that archeologists had ever uncovered, alongside Pompeii, near Naples, and, on the Turkish coast, the vast ruins of Ephesus. Around 200 CE the city was part of the vast Roman Empire, at the height of its power at that time, which extended from Andalusia to the Euphrates, and from Morocco to Syria. When a traveler arrived in the merchant republic of Palmyra, a Greek or Italian trader on horseback, an Egyptian, a Jew, a magistrate sent by Rome, a Roman publican or soldier—in short, a citizen or subject of the empire—the newcomer immediately realized that he had entered a new world. He heard an unknown language being spoken—a great language of the civilized world, Aramaic—and everywhere he saw inscriptions in mysterious writing.

Every rich person he encountered knew Greek, which was the English of that time, but the person's name had guttural consonances that were difficult to grasp or to pronounce. Many local residents weren't dressed like other inhabitants of the Roman Empire. Their clothing wasn't draped, but sewn like our modern clothing, and men wore wide trousers: outfits for hunting and fighting that looked a lot like those of the Persians, the legendary enemies of Rome. This was because, as an author of that time wrote, Rome and Persia "had divided up the world" on either side of the Euphrates River. Those noble Palmyrene horsemen, lords of import-export, wore daggers at their waists, defying the prohibition against carrying weapons on one's person that was imposed on all citizens. The women wore full-length tunics and cloaks that concealed only their hair; they wore embroidered bands around their heads, with twisted turbans on top. Others, however, wore voluminous pantaloons. Their faces weren't veiled, as was the custom in a few regions of the Hellenic world. And so much jewelry! Some even wore a ring on the middle part of their little finger! They may have been in the heart of the desert, but everything exuded wealth. There were statues everywhere, but they were made of bronze, not marble; in the great temple the columns had gilded bronze capitals.

To the south, and to the west as far as the eye could see, the desert, until quite recently, was scattered with a great number of ostentatious monuments, funerary temples, hypogea, or multistory rectangular towers (figures 2 and 3). These were the mausoleums where the great families, those who managed part of the trade between the Roman Empire and Persia, India, and China, buried their dead (whereas the Greco-Roman custom was cremation).

To the north, outside the city, the visitor might have noticed strange beasts: camel caravans were stationed around large warehouses; one sensed that nomadism was not far off. When the visitor's gaze turned back to the city and to the palm grove with its olive trees and vineyards, the massive sanctuary of the Temple of Bel, the patron god of this land, towered above the single-level houses—a sure sign, like the sight of a minaret for Westerners today, that one had indeed entered a new civilization. This Temple of Bel, recently destroyed in our own time, rose up at the end of a long colonnade, which for a moment reassured the visitor because it seemed to belong to the "true" civilization; and at first the shape of the temple itself was reassuring, as it resembled that of all temples in the empire. Its details were also familiar; it spoke the customary architectural vocabulary of columns. The newcomer was familiar with the shape of its Corinthian capitals, and its Ionic capitals, a bit old-fashioned in 200 CE, were thus nothing out of the ordinary.

But when studied more closely, the building was disconcerting: the visitor discovered that it was the bizarre temple of a foreign god. The monumental entrance was not at the front, as would have been logical: it was surprisingly placed on one of the long sides. The top of the building was heavily crenellated (figures 4 and 5), something seen only in the Orient. And it had windows; a temple with windows, just like those in the houses of humans, had never been seen before. Most surprising was that instead of having a roof with two sloping sides, as did all temples, it was covered with a terrace—again, just like a private dwelling. In this region people went up to the roof terrace to eat, feast, or pray to the divinity at the risk of falling off, as did a young man, according to the Acts of the Apostles.

Without doubt the visitor had seen a great deal, and his sense of normalcy was shaken: in the Roman Empire, or rather the Greco-Roman Empire, everything was uniform: architecture, houses, written language and writing, clothing, values, classical authors, and religion, from Scotland to the Rhine, the Danube, the Euphrates, and the Sahara, at least among the elite. Palmyra was indeed a city, a civilized and even cultured place, but it was dangerously close to nomadic noncivilization and a civilization of "the other," that of Persia or of an even more remote place. And the visitor would begin to make generalizations: "Syrians are a nasty breed, a *kakon genos,"* as a Roman or Byzantine soldier in garrison had engraved on a rock in a very busy place. The visitor was mistaken: Palmyra was not a Syrian city like others, just as Venice, in contact with Byzantine and Turkish civilization, was not representative of all of Italy.

2

A Monumental Ancient City

I will now assume my former role as history professor; that is, as a time-traveling tourist guide.

Today, to get to Palmyra it takes four hours by plane from Paris to Damascus, then you have to travel two hundred kilometers on a paved road that noticeably follows the traces of an ancient route; at the end of those four hours traveling through a desert of dry and rocky land where sparse, short, and shriveled grass grows, the appearance of the green palm grove and the white colonnade, an immense vestige of a vanished world, is a surprise of which one never grows tired. Upon arriving, visitors do not discover the "lost jewels of ancient Palmyra" about which Baudelaire dreamed (almost no jewels have been found), but a modern town with hotels and restaurants in a range of prices.

When a visitor turns around, facing away from the town, the horizon is blocked by an astonishing array of half-crumbling constructions (figure 1) with cubes and columns made of white limestone (there is no marble in Syria) against the backdrop of the desert and palm groves. It seems a giant child had fun building 1.5 kilometers of monumental walls and colonnades that are lined up as if marching in a parade; all around one sees scattered pieces that have fallen from the constructions. The impression is not that of ruins, but of a city that has been taken apart: there are no shapeless masses of Roman concrete (as are often found in Rome itself); no arches, either; no curves, only horizontal and vertical lines. It is an architecture of massive stones whose transparent logic is intellectually satisfying: the visitor has the impression that he is seeing all the elements necessary to reconstruct in his mind that which once existed; the structure is the same as the visible shape, all elements creating a single piece.

On the archeological site, no modern construction can be seen; time has stopped here once and for all. What is most striking for the contemporary visitor is what already struck the ancient traveler: a huge sanctuary, today blasted apart, and a long colonnade, those "streets of Palmyra, those forests of columns in the desert plains" about which Hölderlin dreamed as a child. Trade with the outside world had transfigured this Aramean oasis, just as it would turn a few muddy islands on the Adriatic into Venice. The colonnade represented avant-garde urbanism and everyday life in Palmyra; the Temple of Bel was the San Marco of this desert port.

The temple was not a monumental reliquary or a shrine, as temples were in Greece and Rome; equipped with windows, it was the home where Bel lived and where his statue sat on a throne as the saint of all saints. The building rose up in the middle of a rectangular enclosure more than two hundred meters on each side; looking inward at the four sides, this enclosure was a quadrilateral with porticoes (let's call them overhangs) supported by columns; from the exterior, one saw almost windowless walls that protected the temple (just as the admirable mosques of Istanbul remain separated from the city in their large courtyards). Neither the enclosure nor its size was exceptional: wherever the available space allowed, Palmyrenes chose to surround their temples with walls of that type.

The overhangs were not just ornamental or used as shelters against the sun; they offered pilgrims an indispensable campground. Here, merchants sold religious objects that could be offered to the god as ex-votos, and also, I imagine, poultry, which those of lesser means could offer up as sacrifices. On the back wall, devout pilgrims engraved in the plaster the written proof of their visit to the temple, or their thanks to the god who had answered their prayers. And of course, the vast enclosure must have been full during the annual celebration of the god.

Who financed this monumental construction? We don't know. There are three possible answers: it might have been built from the commercial profits obtained on the Silk Road, built from the donations of the many pious pilgrims, or financed by the Roman imperial family. The rich faithful, for example, might have offered one or two columns, following a custom that was common at that time. An emperor or an imperial prince might have gifted a column to the city when it became part of the empire. Or perhaps the treasure of the temple itself was used; the gods received gifts and bequests, and priests were entitled to a portion of the sacrificed animals, which they later resold: temples were competitors of the local butcher shops. Or perhaps the temple was the goal of a regional pilgrimage that attracted a crowd of faithful from afar; if it was widely famous it might have received donations or bequests of real estate, from which it reaped the profits. (Perhaps miracles were not as great as they appeared.)

Just the temple was consecrated in 32 CE; the enclosure and its porticoes must have been constructed only gradually, over decades. Many other pagan or Christian sanctuaries were completed over centuries. The temple itself is not that big. Granted, Syria was quite fond of all things large (it was one of the wealthiest provinces of the empire, along with Tunisia and eastern Turkey), and the temple that crowds of tourists visit in Baalbek, Libya, is one of the largest of the ancient world. But the dimensions of Bel's temple in Palmyra were those of normal temples, of the Maison Carrée in Nimes or the temple in Magnesia on the Maeander, in Turkey, which also has eight columns in front and fifteen on the sides, and which was paid for by that small city.

As for the long colonnade (whose path was not paved in stone), today it crosses the entire site, from the Temple of Bel to the ruins of the "baths of Diocletian." This double line of columns that rise up to the heavens and no longer support anything was completed over two centuries (figures 12 and 13). The first section started at the great temple and was a sacred pathway; every year at the spring equinox a procession accompanied an image of Bel, enclosed in a case of red leather and carried by a camel, to a sanctuary in the countryside; women watched the procession go by with their faces and entire bodies wrapped in veils, either out of respect for the god or because they were in a public place. The later sections of the colonnade had a secondary function: they were lined with shops installed under the porticoes.

The colonnade was not a normal road. One mustn't imagine caravans traveling along it; they certainly did not enter the city. Along part of the great avenue was the souk of Palmyra, "the portico under which everything was sold," as it was called, and the place where people strolled. The souk had regular geometrical dimensions which conformed to the rational design of an advanced civilization, and which formed a contained space: a place where one went, rather than a passageway to somewhere else. Souks, and such use of public space, are unknown in the Western world.

Another example of this: in every ancient city, large or small, the circulation of private conveyances and horseback riders was forbidden. Only wagons carrying goods were allowed to enter the city; individuals left their mounts and their carriages outside the city walls. However, the streets were often encumbered by herds of livestock that passed through, to be slaughtered for the consumption of the city dwellers. Every morning many of those city dwellers left the city and, in the evening, hurried to return before the city gates were shut; they had spent the day working in the fields.

What was most amazing about the colonnade is that it was a civil monument; and so Palmyra was a true city-state, following the Greco-Roman concept. This was a new idea in Syria, which had known only royal, religious, or funerary edifices: surrounding walls and gates, temples, palaces, and tombs. Large-scale urbanism became widespread only in the Roman period. We should mention how popular colonnades truly were. It was probably Antioch, the capital of Syria, that was the first city to have these avenues with paved streets that were lined with "hundreds of columns, all of the same diameter, the ornaments of some insipid rue de Rivoli," wrote Renan, who liked neither that classical urbanism nor Bonaparte.[3]

In Syria, those imperious colonnades formed the axis of a future space arranged on a geometric grid; in Palmyra, which was constructed gradually and without a guiding plan, the long line of columns ultimately went through the entire city; outside Syria, colonnaded streets do not normally occupy such a clearly imperative position. These avenues were called *plateia,* or "wide roads," from which French derived *place* [square] and Italian *piazza.* One of those "wide" roads was the *via lata* in Rome, the via del Corso; two kilometers long and lined with shops under porticoes, it went through the exclusive northern part of the city, leading to the Forum, and is still today the axis of Rome.

As in Rome and elsewhere, in Palmyra the columns or pillars of the avenue supported porticoes, and under those overhangs there were doors that each opened onto a shop; in Palmyra, the brick walls of the shops deteriorated over time, leaving only their backbone, the colonnade. Some of those shops were also used as dwellings; others were one-room commercial spaces, as could be seen not long ago in the souk of Damascus. There were curriers, cobblers, makers of inflated animal skins who sent their wares to the Euphrates, where they were used to create rafts loaded with merchandise (following an immemorial technique that had been adopted as far as the Rhone River).

From what we have learned, shopkeepers and tenants paid rent to the city or to a temple treasury, depending on who owned the building. If the shop was that of a cobbler who lived off his daily earnings, it also served as his lodgings for the night, I imagine, as in Pompeii, Herculaneum, and even, only fifty years ago, in old Naples. If it was that of a goldsmith—in Palmyra there was a goldsmith guild, and one for silversmiths as well—he probably had a house in the city.

In addition to a marketplace, a city worthy of the name had to have a public space, a forum, an agora; Palmyra had one (figure 7), and it appears to have followed a guiding architectural principle: its columns rise up perfectly straight, it boasts four porticoes, and it is decorated with two hundred official statues. It would be interesting to know whether the heart of the city beat in this public structure, as happened in other Greco-Roman cities, or whether the buzzing sounds of social life were heard around one of the gates in the city walls, as had been occurring in Oriental cities for three thousand years, and which tourists can still see in Marrakech today.

But where was the city itself? Where did the inhabitants live? So far we have only been talking about monuments. Excavations to the north of the city have revealed streets and homes that were more or less lined up between the great colonnade and the current town. The remains of a few houses can still be seen. Some appear to have been homes of wealthy proprietors, similar to the type of private home that was common throughout the empire, in Ephesus as well as in Vaison-la-Romaine in France or in Pompeii: a single-level dwelling, very long and wide, spreading out over hundreds of square meters, opening onto a central courtyard surrounded by porticoes; mosaics no doubt decorated the ground and the walls, as in the house of Cassiopeia (figure 11), with its beautiful, voluptuous nude with a sad gaze, reflecting the humanist tradition of Greek art.

Other houses sheltered a more modest bourgeoisie. From the exterior their layout is similar, but a few details indicate that life was lived differently in them; two identical doors opened onto two well-separated areas of the home, one where guests were admitted, and one where the women lived, and which was off limits to anyone else. Reflecting wealth or more modest means, these homes had only rare openings onto the exterior. The streets thus resembled those of an old Muslim or Greco-Roman city such as Pompeii, where, away from the commercial street, one passed between two practically windowless walls.

The architectural layout of this northern area appears to have had a geometrical design: that of a grid, but one that was carried out haphazardly, with inexact perpendicular lines and an approximate parallelism. One imagines that preexisting constructions,[4] temples and private dwellings, were later more or less connected by a network of streets. Clearly, this area was first occupied by scattered structures. Was it an encampment of nomads that had no preconceived layout—each individual pitching his tent, being careful to remain at a certain distance from his neighbors—or was the city laid out on a grid, as we see in many American cities? For more than five hundred years Mediterranean cities had been strictly geometrical; at least in the fourth century, this was the case in the Persian quarter in Beirut. This orthogonal layout was that of the cities that had been founded by Greece and of those that Rome implanted everywhere, from Bavay to Carpentras in France, to as far as Timgad, on the edge of the Sahara in Algeria. An ancient city such as Athens seduced tourists with its mazelike streets. Palmyra wanted to be modern, and, at that time, Greek civilization was de rigueur.

Palmyra was foreign to that civilization only by dint of its past, its Aramaic language, its society, its caravan activity, its religion, and many different customs. However, with the layout of its houses, the architecture of its monuments, and its quality of life—in short, for the respect that its wealth inspired—it was on a par with the global civilization: the Palmyrenes were not barbarians and didn't want to be. And so in Syria, the more important a building, the more Hellenized it was. Only Greek architecture was conceivable.

The population of the entire Palmyrene city must have been only in the tens of thousands; other Palmyrenes lived scattered throughout the vast rural territory that belonged to the city. Let's remember that at that time the entire Italian peninsula had only six million inhabitants. As long as a society could survive only if three-quarters of its members worked the land to feed the population, the largest urban areas, such as wealthy Venice in the sixteenth century, rarely reached 150,000 inhabitants. A huge metropolis such as ancient Rome (500,000 inhabitants, or double that) was the exception, as would be other world capitals—London or Edo (the future Tokyo), with their million inhabitants, or Istanbul or Paris—in the eighteenth century.

An ancient city and its surrounding land formed an administrative and economic unit, of which the city was, so to speak, the capital. The surface area of the whole was closer to that of a French *département* than to that of a French *commune*.[5] In Palmyra a long, bilingual inscription called the "Palmyrene Tariff" informs us that upon entering the city, a tax, or *octroi*, would be levied on merchandise coming in "from outside the borders" of the city, including slaves, courtesans, and perfume, but not on provisions coming from the "villages" of the region. However, water was a luxury commodity: a very high annual tax was imposed on irrigation using the springs of the oasis.

Life must have been expensive in Palmyra, because its surrounding territory was not sufficient to provide it with everything it needed, unlike most other ancient cities, which couldn't have survived otherwise. It drew salt from the lagoons of the desert, and resold it, but had to import other necessary goods such as wheat, wine, and oil—the trinity of Mediterranean lands—which it did not produce in sufficient quantities. The land was better suited to raising goats and sheep for the consumption of the city dwellers, camels for the caravans, and horses for the armed guards who escorted them. Palmyra also imported *garum*, similar to Vietnamese *nuoc-mâm*: fermented fish sauce, a common condiment in ancient Middle Eastern and Asian cuisine.

Like every ancient city, Palmyra did have a vast territory

(to the west and the Syrian coast, its borders were seventy kilometers away). The city and the palm grove were not right in the middle of the desert, but close to its border; and so the Palmyrene territory was essentially located in the critical zone containing two hundred millimeters of rainwater that made farming and livestock husbandry possible. In the areas closest to the city, the groundwater was collected through underground canalization, accessible by wells that were scattered over the area. To the east and toward the Euphrates was the desert, but to the north, archeologists have discovered villages of livestock farmers whose unfired brick houses were topped with terraces, villages with entire cistern systems. Palmyra's other large rural zone was around fifty kilometers to the south; it was irrigated by a large Roman-era dam capable of holding 140,000 cubic meters of water.

Let's linger a moment on these rural expanses and the villagers who lived there. They made up a different population than that of the city. Greek was unknown there; only Aramaic, which would survive the imposition of Greek, was spoken and written. Hellenization was much more important for the inhabitants of cities than for those living in the countryside.

The civilization of pagan antiquity was an urban phenomenon, fed by a huge peasantry that remained on the fringes of urban life; "What good can come from Nazareth?" was said to those who announced that a messiah (whose language was Aramaic, by the way) had been born there. This division would come to an end four or five centuries later, when the Christian and Muslim sides of the Mediterranean were each dominated by a religious culture that admitted no culture other than its own; each person would henceforth identify himself (with a "color," the Koran would say) as Christian, Muslim, or Jew.

And so we can understand what the word "city" meant in antiquity. Because the large majority of inhabitants that made up the population of an urban territory worked the land, the city proper was inhabited mainly by landowners who spent what they earned off their land there, by their large number of domestic servants, and by the shopkeepers who provided goods and services to them and to the peasants of the territory.

But what about the poor? Where did they live? The urban poor were the masses of domestic help that filled the homes of the wealthy. The truly poor did not live in the city; they were the poverty-stricken peasants. A city was scarcely a kilometer in diameter (or even half; rarely twice that), and a large part of that surface area was covered with public buildings, temples, the hammam (Turkish bath), and buildings intended for various performances. Statues were everywhere: those of emperors, of benefactors of the city—the center of power and a showcase of civilization and urban life.

3

Being a Capitalist Back Then

The oasis of Palmyra was also a commercial center where peasants from the surrounding countryside would come to sell their wares before going to the souk for their own provisions. The private homes of the regional landowners occupied the rest of the space. But here is what made Palmyra unique: the beautiful homes there were inhabited not by the landowners but by the agents of the caravan business. Palmyrenes, wrote an ancient historian, "as they are a trading people, . . . bring Indian or Arabian products from Persia, and market them in Roman territory."[6]

From Arabia and the Orient, Rome indeed imported goods that were not very heavy but were in high demand: not the heavy cargo of grain or minerals but bundles of incense for all the sanctuaries of the empire, myrrh, pepper, ivory, pearls, and Indian or Chinese fabrics (bits of Chinese cotton and silk have been found in the tombs of Palmyra, where the bodies were often mummified). The lovely Roman women wore robes of silk more revealing than if their wearers were naked; moralists and poets railed against them. But even men, and above all senators, ultimately adopted silk clothing.

The largest amount of imported goods probably ended up in Alexandria. Palmyra shared the rest with Petra, the Jordanian tourist site that was no less illustrious, located on the ancient "incense road," and, to the north, Batnaya, a religious center and the site of a great annual fair (these always went hand in hand), where central Asia and the Silk Road with its two-humped camels went into the Roman province of Anatolia.

This sumptuous commerce was scorned by moralists and by those who criticized Rome for importing goods rather than just focusing on exporting; what was imported, however, did not amount to very much on an imperial scale (it might have represented 0.5 percent of the gross national product). But it was enough to make a handful of specialized importers rich, those who thereby earned a revenue equal to what several hundred thousands of inhabitants might earn. Their profit came from the huge gap between the buying price and the selling price: our sources, a Latin naturalist and a Chinese informant, speak of goods that were sold for ten or even a hundred times more than their purchase price. For various reasons we cannot provide the current monetary value of the ancient prices, but here is something that is very telling: a third of a kilo of raw silk from China sold for the price of tens of thousands of eggs or of six thousand haircuts, or for sixteen months of a farm worker's salary, not counting what he paid for food. The average cost of living and salaries in the empire were those of the current third world, with a gap (like the one we currently know of) between mass poverty and enormous fortunes, which were sources of authority and respect. Let's hazard a comparison with the salary of the average Palmyrene: they would have earned forty euros per month on average, or half that, or double that, but not ten times that.

At the time when Palmyra was at the height of its glory, a Chinese informant was sent westward and arrived in Syria. "The inhabitants are honest in business and there are no double prices," he reported, adding that commercial profit was tenfold. But, he says, the Persians "want to continue to sell their Chinese silk and this is why these inhabitants are cut off from all direct communication with the Chinese." And so Palmyra looked to Persia for its treasures from India and Arabia, and those treasures got there by two routes: by boat on the Persian Gulf, or via the Silk Road.

On the route that led from the Euphrates to Punjab and the Huáng Hé or Yellow River, there were excavations in Bagram, Afghanistan, not far from Kabul, that revealed what must have been the palace of an Indo-Scythian potentate. Archeologists found a cache of objects that were probably left in passing by great trade caravans: Indian ivory; Chinese lacquer; Syrian painted glass; lamps; small, grotesque bronzes in the Alexandrine style (a statuette of Hercules-Serapis, or the caricature of a philosopher); glass painted with the image of the beacon of Alexandria; plaster medallions with figurative motifs: mythological scenes, gladiator battles, and various curiosities. What is striking is the relative lack of value of this charming collection, and the care with which these objects had been meticulously preserved in a well-sealed place; it might be possible that passing caravans had left them as ex-votos to the god of a temple along the way, of whom they became the sacred and untouchable property.

As for the sea route, it left from the base of the Persian Gulf and, with the help of the monsoon, led to a trading center located at the mouth of the Indus, near Karachi, Pakistan; then it traveled south along the Indian peninsula to Ceylon (Sri Lanka), then back up to the outskirts of Pondicherry, where spices and silk could be traded for wine, Syrian glass, and beautiful red glazed pottery made in Arezzo, Tuscany—a common, everyday type of vessel that became expensive only because of how far it had traveled. Once back from their expeditions, which might have lasted between one and several years, sailors and traders told of what they had learned on their travels: Rome came to know of the existence of the Great Wall.

Palmyra's role in all this was to help get the merchandise over the 1,300 kilometers, as the crow flies, that separated the cities and ports of Syria from the Persian Gulf and the sea route, by crossing the Syrian desert to the welcoming banks of the Euphrates and the fertile Persian territory; this was the annual adventure of the large caravans. The bartering and palavers with tribal chiefs and the bribing of the Roman and Persian customs officers were done in Greek and in Aramaic, the international languages of business.

We can see what made Palmyra so prosperous: it is located on the shortest path between the Mediterranean and the blue waters of the Euphrates; this path was only a road in the rocky desert. But Palmyrenes were technicians of the desert: those camel drivers knew how to cross its three or four hundred kilometers from one water source to the next, a difficult journey in summer, and one that was threatened by attacks from nomads. Let's not forget that their camels had one hump and were, "on account of their great speed, called dromedaries," wrote Saint Jerome;[7] rare animals, they had just recently been introduced into North Africa.

But there is something more important: The Palmyrenes were able to build a commercial empire from what might have been merely transport services; they themselves bought and then resold what they were transporting; traders were part of the caravans. What is more, some of them armed the ships on the Red Sea, thereby competing with their Egyptian rivals. Palmyra was not just a caravan city; it was a merchant republic.

Several routes led from Palmyra to the Euphrates en route to the gulf; aerial archeology has enabled us to see one. The flint stone that was placed to support the camels' feet formed two parallel strips twelve to eighteen meters apart, so low that they are visible only from above under low-angle lighting. Once on the banks of the Euphrates, one could cross the river by ferry, but the caravans probably opted for the river route, using rafts made of inflated animal skins. Waterways in antiquity were what the railroads became in modern times.

The Euphrates offered a choice between two commercial routes, one upstream, the other downstream. One could either go up on the river or on its banks to Seleucia on the Tigris, a large Greek city on Persian land, a victorious rival of Babylon and a commercial center where imports from Asia flowed in; or one could go down the river and land at what has been called the Hong Kong of those times: Charax Spasinu, at the head of the Persian Gulf, not far from the modern border between Iraq and Kuwait.

At a location on their journey, in Vologesias, a city located somewhere on the Euphrates, the Palmyrenes had a relay station on Persian territory: they had a trading post, a caravanserai, a *khan*, a *fonduk*, both inn and warehouse, where they enjoyed a de facto exterritoriality. And so a magnate from Palmyra, Soados, raised a temple there to divinized Roman emperors.

Going back up the river, one might also find Palmyrene merchants who negotiated with their Greek counterparts in Seleucia on the Tigris; they could obtain beautiful silks there, sure to appeal to a lasting clientele (more than one saint of the future Christian Gaul would have silk from Persia for his shroud). But most caravans went downstream toward Charax and the Gulf. The expedition probably occurred in the winter months, since in summer the Persian Gulf is one of the hottest regions in the world. The round-trip journey lasted several months, depending on the season and what might happen along the way. Each voyage was a momentous event in a caravan driver's life; and when his caravan driving days were over, a driver could proudly count how many times he had gone to the Gulf.

A few bilingual inscriptions in Greek and Aramaic provide eloquent testimony of the importance of such events. In one, the pious benefactor Saodos in 145 CE is honored with a statue "for having saved from the great danger that threatened the caravan that was returning from Vologesias." I imagine that he rushed to its rescue at the head of his men.

In another inscription, the wealthy Taimarsu in the year 193 received a statue from the caravan leaders who "went up" with him from Charax, because he had paid the sum of three hundred "gold coins" as travel expenses for them. Such was the importance and probably the authority of rich benefactors. Charax was the hub of Palmyrene commercial traffic because the gulf was the meeting place of Oriental traders. This region—inhabited by "Arabs," which meant nomads—thus formed a small kingdom. A curious thing: the local potentates there had conferred important functions, political powers, on the Palmyrenes. This was less under the pressure of an economic imperialism, I imagine, than by virtue of a maxim that is not exclusively Oriental: Confer important missions only upon foreigners to avoid any collusion with local powers. A Palmyrene was thus named satrap, or governor, of what is today the oil emirate of Bahrain. And so Palmyra was considered a breeding ground for able wielders of power.

In addition to the large annual caravans whose terminus was the gulf, some Palmyrene traders hazarded a longer journey, as far as the markets located at the mouth of the Indus, where they set off with their merchandise. We have found the tomb of one of those traders, upon which he had himself represented in front of the ship, a large, stocky vessel with square sails, armed with a ramming device to defend against pirates and equipped with a lateral rudder.

Then it was time to return. When the caravans had "come back up" from the Gulf and returned to Palmyra, the adventure was practically over. Important things happened in Palmyra. First, there was Roman customs, which seems to have taxed imports at a quarter of their value; where could the customs post have been set up if not in Palmyra itself, an obligatory point of passage where Rome had placed a military garrison as a means to suppress contraband? But most important, the sale of many of the imported goods had been negotiated and carried out en route by the Palmyrenes themselves, who, from being caravan leaders, thus became traders.

Just north of Palmyra and outside the city limits, Jean-Marie Dentzer[8] identified from aerial photos a whole group of structures whose layout is bizarre: these were commercial warehouses, "docks," caravanserais, or *khans*. So the caravans did not enter the city, which was better for hygiene and traffic; they didn't have to pay the municipal octroi of the tariff.

The final stage of the journey, within the province of Syria and under the protection of Roman troops, was not dangerous or difficult. The same was not true of the return through the desert no man's land between the Euphrates and Palmyra, where the caravan needed an armed escort. The problem wasn't one of water (water sources weren't rare, because in the Syrian desert the precious liquid could be obtained at a fairly shallow depth), but of looters.

As Saint Jerome later wrote: "On the road from Beroa to Edessa adjoining the high-way is a waste over which the Saracens roam to and fro without having any fixed abode. Through fear of them travellers [*sic*] in those parts assemble in numbers, so that by mutual assistance they may escape impending danger."[9] In the desert or on the steppes, being alone was perilous; marauders rose up on the roads to rob their victims and turn them into slaves. To come out of the desert alive was a gift for which one thanked the gods. In the desert of what is now Jordan, nomads—the Bedouins of that time—carved tens of thousands of graffiti in archaic Arabic in which they invoke their warrior goddess in these terms: "O Allat, security and spoils," "O Allat, vengeance," "O Allat, security to he who mounts the guard." Piracy of the land was considered a normal practice, along with livestock raising and a bit of agriculture.

And so the annual caravan or caravans and their long months of traveling was not an easy undertaking; they required men, animals, capital, organization, and leaders. Regarding capital, here is an interesting detail. In those times, they used shards or debris from walls as scratch paper. On the wall of a funerary tower, an unknown Palmyrene thus did his accounting in Aramaic: In one month he had earned 2,236 coins on his loans, at 30 percent it seems, which would mean that the loan rate for caravans equaled that of so-called risky maritime loans. Caravan expeditions thus involved capitalists; they also involved traders, as we have seen.

The expedition itself was placed under the authority of a caravan leader whose title the Palmyrenes had forged from the Greek word "synodiarch." But those men were not the true masters of the enterprise; they were only responsible for how the expedition was actually carried out. The lords of the caravan economy were those whom we call magnates, Soados, or that Iarhai who was honored with twelve statues (which was a lot, even at that time when an average city had one official statue per some thousand inhabitants; in Palmyra it was probably one per one hundred . . .). These men didn't take part in the expeditions, or did not necessarily do so, but they had the capital and, what is more, the human resources necessary to carry them out.

They represented a type of entrepreneur who was unique to those times and that place. It was a type quite different from the one Max Weber discovered at the origins of modern capitalism—that is, the Protestant business man, a man of duty, picturesque with his long face, and whom, invoking André Gide, we might call a *Profitendieu*. The Palmyrene capitalist was a horseman, a warrior, a sheik, as Ernest Will writes in an insightful article: the de facto chief of the more or less sedentary tribes of the Palmyrene territory and the desert.[10] It was thanks to him that Palmyra was able to bring its commercial potential to fruition; his authority and audacity made use of competent caravan leaders. The same armed resources might explain the era of Zenobia challenging Rome as a pretender to the imperial throne.

It is not likely an exaggeration to state that this Aramean city, with its networks of clans, of clientele and lineages, was unlike any other Syrian city. It resembled less a city of the empire than it did other merchant cities like Mecca or Medina in the time of Mohammed (who, in his youth, took part in caravans). Like those Arabian cities, Palmyra was structured not around a civic body, but rather around a group of tribes, and it was dominated by a few families of merchant princes. The magnates of Palmyra, proud of an authority that gave them license to pursue bold undertakings, could take advantage of their dual culture: without humility or resentment, they were on equal footing with the Hellenic culture, they knew the wider world, they measured it, but they maintained the power to raise among their followers a private army to defend Rome or, on the contrary, to attack it.

The Romans were well aware of the armed might that could arise out of the desert; they were wary of it at home and they used it abroad. Palmyra was overseen by a unit of Roman cavalry initially recruited from among the locals of Thrace, now Bulgaria, which was followed by a unit formed from the Vocontii in Vaison-la-Romaine, the seat of the canton in the Vaucluse *département* which was at that time the regional capital and center of the Romanization of a large territory, that of the rugged mountain dwellers of the Dauphiné province.

4

Antiquity in Antiquity

Such, then, was Palmyra, and such were its inhabitants around the year 100 or 200 CE, when the monuments of the Roman era, which we could see until recently, were built. But to understand the "why" of Palmyra, we must go back at least another thousand years, to a quite different world, to an antiquity within antiquity, around 1000 BCE—to the time of the Assyrians, of Babylon, of the Phoenicians, of King David, who founded Jerusalem, and of the legendary Trojan War—when Gaul was not yet *gauloise*.

In those distant times, Palmyra had already existed for many thousands of years—that is, for four thousand years, all told—and it already had a name: Tadmor, the Arabic name that is used today and which is found on local maps. But from that very distant past we know only of its name; so let us remain at around 1000 BCE. A massive upheaval was occurring in that period: a nomadic people whose name appeared then for the first time, the Arameans, gradually invaded Syria, and gave it their name: Aram. "Twenty-eight times," wrote an Assyrian king in his annals, "I have battled the Arameans of Tadmor."

In vain: Syrians, as well as the inhabitants of Mesopotamia, stopped speaking Aramaic only when they began speaking Arabic, even though between 539 BCE and the Muslim conquest in 636 CE the Syrian territory was occupied by the Persians, then by the Greeks, heirs of Alexander the Great, and finally by the Romans. We mustn't be too distraught at the thought of those foreign dominations; for much of the ancient world, it was fairly common to obey a foreign master—or rather, the "nationality" of the master was of little importance.

Aramaic had long served as an international and diplomatic language from Syria and Iran to Afghanistan. It later ceased to be used for writing, and was replaced for that purpose by the Greek of the conquerors, but it remained the language spoken by the majority of the Syrian population up until the Muslim conquest. It was adopted by everyone: by the Arabs, who continued to infiltrate Syria for many long centuries, and by the Jews, who abandoned Hebrew (some of the last books of their Bible are in Aramaic). It survived Greek, the lofty language of scholars, whose role it would one day assume, while the Gaulish language disappeared without a trace. When Syria became Christian, the rich Syriac literature dealt in Aramaic with the greatest philosophical and theological subjects in Hellenic thought, which up until then had only been the purview of Greek.

Palmyrenes were thus Aramaens, with some Arab elements, who continued to speak Aramaic at home, as did all Syrians, but who also continued to write it at the same time as Greek; their lavish family mausoleums often have bilingual inscriptions at the door, but inside the tomb the epitaph of each deceased is only in Aramaic; the dual languages attested to the interest the family had in the wider world.

The Palmyra whose history we know best is the one that Rome, already the master of the rest of Syria, had annexed around the beginning of the Christian era; it is the city of the first three centuries CE, the one we could see, with its ruins and its two thousand inscriptions (several hundred in Greek, and a dozen or so in Arabic). But it is possible to imagine what it was before the birth of Christ: for centuries, or even millennia, Palmyra was that well-known and unique city, "Tadmor of the desert," that the Biblical author of Chronicles knew well around 400 BCE. The oasis with its sulfurous or potable springs was probably inhabited by sedentary farmers and herders. We know the names of at least seventeen tribes for whom Palmyra was their hub; they built their seasonal camps there. We can imagine a city of constructions made of rammed earth and bricks dried in the sun. It is likely that the city that would later emerge was formed by the gathering of a certain number of tribes, both Aramean and Arab; Maurice Sartre has shown that the cities of Hauran and of the Druze djebel were formed in this way.[11]

Each tribe maintained its ancestral sanctuary, and the many divinities, accepted by all, coexisted peacefully, even when two tribes were in conflict. In 32 CE the Temple of Bel was consecrated; and around the same time, three other Syrian cities—Baalbek, Gerasa (modern Jerash), and Petra—constructed or reconstructed their great sanctuaries, which cannot be a mere coincidence: civic pride was a sensitive subject, cities were jealous of each other, spied on each other, and were rivals in their architectural achievements. Public buildings brought "beauty and grandeur" to cities, as was quite openly proclaimed.

Three centuries later, Christian emperors would forbid the destruction of the pagan temples, as they were considered ornaments of the conquered cities.

5

Palmyra: A Subject of the Caesars

The first few decades of the Christian era saw another great event: the annexation to the Roman Empire of that tempting prey, Palmyra, which until then had remained independent of Rome, as it had no doubt been of the Greek kings of Syria. The Romans must have tried to make the trafficking in contraband more difficult by placing their customs post in a place where caravans seeking a water source and a caravanserai would necessarily stop. International politics must also have come into play. The desert was a political vacuum. Since the Persian territory stopped at the Euphrates, the desert did belong to Rome, but only as nominally as the western part of the North American continent belonged to the United States before Western expansion. To conquer Palmyra and install a garrison there was to reassert the empire's rights over the desert. Palmyra would become part of the Roman Empire, and then the Byzantine Empire, until the Muslim conquest.

Having become a subject of the Caesars, and following a general practice, the city soon consecrated a monument to the divinized emperors whose architecture was, however, more honorific than religious, because worshiping the emperors was an obvious display of loyalty that no one dreamed of taking literally. Further, in the year 75 at the latest (our documentation is sparse), in public decrees the city designated

itself a "city-state" or *polis*—that is, a collectivity organized
around the model of a Greek or even Roman city. It was gov-
erned by a president or *proedros*, a council, an assembly of
the people, two magistrates (who were replaced every year)
called archontes, and a secretary of the council and the people (who, under that modest title, represented the city in its
dealings with the Roman governor of the province). However, we mustn't have any illusions about the democratic nature of the regime, in spite of the existence of an "assembly of
the people." As in Greek or Roman cities of that time, the true
masters of the city were the wealthy, the notables.

It is sometimes assumed that in annexing Palmyra, Rome
conferred its political organization upon the city. Is that
indeed true? Palmyra's constitution seems typically Greek,
and could thus be older than its connection to the empire,
going back to the time of the Greek kings of Syria. Further-
more, nothing was more foreign to the Romans' political pru-
dence and lack of proselytism than to modify the customs of
the societies over which they became the masters; they never
sought to spread Roman civilization, which was actually only
two versions of Hellenism: Hellenization in the Greek language in the eastern Mediterranean region, and Hellenization in Latin in the West. They simply considered as civilized
the local oligarchies that, everywhere and spontaneously,
adopted their civic organization and way of life.

Since there is a lot of talk today about cultural imperialism
and national identity, we forget that throughout history, mod-
ernization through the adoption of foreign customs played a
role far more important than nationalism; the culture of the
other was adopted, not as something foreign, but as something considered to be the true way of living, one that could
not be left only to the foreigner who was simply the first to
possess it. Some might fear uniformization; in truth, "foreign"

innovations are continuously born everywhere, and are then spread far and wide.

Civilizations do not have a "fatherland" and have always been without political, religious, or cultural borders to separate the human herds. Nietzsche admired the energy with which the Romans had adopted Greek values as their own. On that part of the planet where Greek was the international language of culture and trade, Hellenism was always the "global" civilization that impressed all peoples, the prestigious foreign model that one imitated, as well as the mirror in which the different peoples believed to see their own reflections in a truer form. To be Hellenized was to remain oneself while becoming more oneself; it was to become modern.

6

A Syrian Tribe and a Hellenized City

Some civilizations have an influence that we cannot explain. History has often disproven that this is due either to cultural imperialism or even to political superiority: the Romans never sought to Romanize or to Hellenize; conquered Greece "conquered its fearsome conqueror," wrote the Roman poet Horace; and, five centuries later, we saw the "Persian conquest of Islam" the conqueror. All the same, under its Greek and civic exterior, Palmyra for a long time retained a half-tribal organization. A Syrian tribe was made up of a certain number of clans or lineages bringing together the male descendants of a real or mythical ancestor whose name the tribe assumed; the members of the tribe were his sons, his *beni*. The Israelites, whose mythical ancestor was Israel, were the *bnei Yisrael* or "sons of Israel," and their ancestral god was Yahweh. Similarly, among the twenty or so tribes in Palmyra, the *Beni Maazin*, apparently of nomadic origin, were the "sons of the goatherd," and their ancestral god was Baalshamin, the "Lord of Heaven(s)" (figure 6).

But it is important to note that the word "tribe" also designated something very different. After a Greek city had been established, it was divided into a determined number of "tribes" or districts into which the citizenry was divided; these electoral "tribes" had the names of legendary heroes

(Erechtheus or Cecrops in Athens, for example). And Palmyra was organized in the same way; the city was officially divided into four "tribes," each of which had its sanctuary, each of which bore the name of its so-called ancestor. And all four of them made up the civic body: the *Beni Mita*; the *Beni Mattabol*; the *Beni Maazin;*, mentioned above, and the *Beni Komare*. In Aramaic the latter were the "Sons of the Priest"; that is, they were priests in that land where a "carpenter's son" was a carpenter and the Son of Man, a man. But earlier they were called the "Sons of *Cohen*," which meant the same thing in Phoenician: a *cohen* was a priest (as in Hebrew).

What was Palmyra like in those early first two centuries: a true city, or a conglomeration of tribes ruled by their respective sheiks? We might easily assume it was essentially a tribal system under the veneer of civic districts.

A minor fact confirms that an abyss had long separated Aramean and Arab societies from other cities of the empire, with their unique oligarchic civil system in which their notables participated: in Palmyra, on more than a thousand epitaphs in Aramaic, the public functions which many wealthy deceased must necessarily have held (that of member of the council, for example, or of aedile or treasurer) are rarely mentioned, whereas their parents and ancestors are meticulously noted, sometimes going back five generations. This is as surprising as it would be if, under the French Ancien Régime, the epitaph of a noble didn't mention his title of nobility, that he had been a count or a duke. Because, throughout the Greek and Roman world, the public functions bestowed by the city, by the little "fatherland," were true titles of nobility; what was important was to have been a praetor, an archon, a duumviri, or simply an advisor to the city; such functions were integral to a notable's identity.

There was nothing like this in Palmyra, where the honors bestowed by the city were less important than the greatness of one's family, for whom such honors were of only minor consequence (let's say in passing that the family was monogamous and also that men often married their cousins, as in the modern Maghreb as described by Germaine Tillion).[12] However, many funerary portraits show individuals wearing sacerdotal insignia on their heads: a cylindrical headpiece in the shape of the base of a mortarboard, or a tall, conical tiara with a band of leaves circling the base, and a medallion or a tiny bust of a god or a divinized emperor in the front. These were priests or members of one of the many private associations whose purpose was to honor a god and to prepare sacred feasts. Clearly, it was more important to be a "head of a sacred banquet" than to be a magistrate; civic-mindedness was not as important as the distinctions that went with demonstrations of piety. In those times, having religion went without saying; that said, every person could have the gods he wanted.

The powers in Rome, informed by their resident in Palmyra or by the governor of Syria, knew that Palmyra largely remained a foreigner, that notables continued to be called Wahballat or Yedibel instead of taking Greek names and calling themselves Athenodoros or Theognostos like everyone else, and as many other Syrians did. This is perhaps why the rich Palmyrenes didn't benefit as much from a favor that was distributed increasingly widely throughout the empire: to be made Roman citizens and thus go from the status of "natives" to that of "metropolitans" (if I may be excused that anachronistic though expedient word)—with some dozen or so exceptions, such as the magnate Iarhai, whose new civil status obliged him henceforth to be called Marcus Ulpius Iaraios, following the Roman custom; at least he saved his Aramean name while tacking on a Greek-sounding suffix. Perhaps, too, the dominant stratum was limited to some dozen magnates and did not form an entire "bourgeois class" of notables— whereas in Roman Asia, almost all the "bourgeoisie" of the Greek cities were Roman citizens by the second century.

7

Saving the Empire

In the third century, profound changes began to occur in Palmyra and also in the Greek Orient. First, around the year 200 Palmyra was suddenly raised to the rank of colony—which, unlike the modern meaning of the word, meant that it had been made the equal of other cities of the Roman "metropolis." And the Palmyrenes assimilated the spirit of that promotion: in their official texts they henceforth proudly included their titles of duumvir, aedile, or advisor, without, however, giving up their bilingual inscriptions or their Aramean names. They were proud to have become true Romans while remaining themselves. Here we see a contrast between two forms of "national" identity. As the much-missed Claude Lepelley kindly pointed out to me, the ambition of Greek cities, unlike those of the Syrians, was never to become Roman cities; quite the opposite. Syrians and Palmyrenes were like other peoples of the empire: like the Gauls, for example, who as Gauls considered themselves members of the Roman Empire.

But the Greeks, not to mention the Jews, always felt like a nation conquered by foreign masters; they continued to contrast "you Romans" with "us Greeks" up to the beginning of the Byzantine era, when, through escheat, they would become masters of what remained of the empire. The Syrians had their national culture, their traditions, their pride, no doubt;

FIGURE 1. Overhead view of Palmyra before May 2015. © Georg Gerster / Rapho.

FIGURE 2. Funerary tower, destroyed in early September 2015. Photo © Johan Siegers.

FIGURE 3. Three Brothers' Hypogeum. Photo © Martin Talbot. CC by 2.0: https://creativecommons.org/licenses/by/2.0/legalcode.

FIGURES 4 AND 5. Temple of Bel, destroyed by ISIS on August 30, 2015. © De Agostini / Leemage.

FIGURE 6. Temple of Baalshamin, destroyed by ISIS on August 23, 2015. Courtesy of Brandt Maxwell.

FIGURE 7. Agora. Courtesy of Brandt Maxwell.

FIGURE 8. Theater. © Michele Falzone / Alamy Stock Photo.

FIGURE 9. Funerary bust of Aqmat, late second century CE. © The Trustees of the British Museum. All rights reserved.

FIGURE 10. Veiled women following a procession (detail from a bas-relief in the Temple of Bel). Photo © Verity Cridland. CC by 2.0: https://creativecommons.org/licenses/by/2.0/legalcode.

FIGURE 11. Mosaic in the House of Cassiopeia (detail), third century CE. © akg-images / Gerard Degeorge.

FIGURE 12. The Great Colonnade. Photo © Dr. Colleen Morgan. CC by 2.0: https://creativecommons.org/licenses/by/2.0/legalcode.

FIGURE 13. Monumental Arch of the Great Colonnade. Photo © Varun Shiv Kapur. CC by 2.0: https://creativecommons.org/licenses/by/2.0/legalcode.

SAVING THE EMPIRE · 39

but they didn't have the intractable cultural nationalism of the Greeks, or their superb disdain for all that came from Rome; they didn't object to belonging to the great empire whose legions protected Syria from Persian invasions. Like everyone else, they had their customs, their traditions, their values, and a fully established identity, but without having a sharp and sensitive awareness of it, without turning it into a holy cause, whereas the phrase "all the Greeks" or "the Hellenics" was enough to satisfy and swell the hearts of the Hellenes.

While reading the inscriptions in Palmyra, one has the impression that in time the city became increasingly familiar with Rome and its institutions, with the complicated hierarchy of its power, and that it became a city like others, a true city of the empire. During the second century, the name of the tribe to which a person belonged stopped being mentioned after the person's given name. In the following century, in the terrible third century, particularisms were retreating everywhere in the face of threats from the outside; Palmyra needed Rome and its legions, and Palmyrenes felt they were members of the empire.

It is important to remember this in order not to see excessive nationalism in an unforeseen episode that brought Palmyra to the forefront of history: the period of conquest by the city in the desert between 259 and 274. Those fifteen years created the fame of Odaenathus and his widow Zenobia, a sort of queen of Palmyra who attempted to seize the Roman throne.

Zenobia's attempt occurred during the worst years the empire had ever experienced. A perfect storm had blown in: there were barbarian invasions along the Rhine and the Danube, while on the Euphrates the Persian kings had shaken the equilibrium that existed between the two empires: the King of Kings could boast on his triumphal inscription of having burned and sacked Syria. It's not clear whether he hoped to conquer the Orient, to raid it, or to deflate Roman pride with his power and that of his gods. The Roman Empire was henceforth only a citadel besieged by the *Germanii* and the Persians.

And inside the citadel there was anarchy: in one generation some thirty emperors fought for power at the cost of their lives. Several of these ephemeral rulers died noble deaths, but one of them died in his bed, the victim of another scourge, the plague. This competition for the throne can be explained. The imperial regime was a unique institution that had nothing in common with a monarchy as we know it, that of the French Ancien Régime, for example; the emperor was an appointed leader, not the owner of his kingdom through hereditary right. There was no automatic rule or process for accession to supreme power; any dedicated citizen, a member of the elite, could lay claim to the title to assure common salvation, regardless of the province he came from, if he had the means to succeed. With such a system, peaceful periods, such as the golden age of the Antonines, could only be the exception to the rule.

And so, from the year 240, the empire, on the verge of collapse, needed more than ever to be saved. The desperate situation in which it found itself gave rise to a panic-stricken patriotic rivalry between different armies: the Imperial Guard, the legions of the Rhine, those of the Danube, and those of Syria. Each wanted to elevate its leader as the best savior. Because Rome then lived under a militaristic regime, the rise in threats to the empire had pushed the emperors, those mandated saviors, to become themselves leaders of their armies and to no longer simply delegate responsibility to their lieutenants. Consequently, the armies henceforth wielded real power and soldiers "made" emperors because the throne was their business: the emperor was dependent on them. The drama at that time was played out through three entities: the emperor, the army, and the empire to be defended—or, as Julian the Apostate would say, between the shepherd, his dogs and the herd. But it was the dogs that chose the right shepherd, and they were rarely in agreement on that.

In the political culture of the soldiers, saving the empire and providing a savior emperor was the affair of the military, which had become the ruling class; but that class wasn't the official army. The entire class was made up of three or four large armies, and it was constituted of that many individuals— and that many rivals. As a result, there were three decades of anarchy when the authentic patriotism of the armies was hardly distinguishable from their mutual jealousies, and which resulted in conflicts among pretenders to the throne. There seemed to be *pronunciamientos*, or deaths of "usurpers," once every year.

Any emperor who lost a battle or was judged to be inept had lost his mandate as savior, which was his true legitimacy, and was often put to death by his own soldiers. Every general who conquered the barbarians was, sometimes against his will, proclaimed emperor by his troops, who identified with their leader while other armies pitted their own generals against him. After the battle, the fortunate elected one ostensibly proclaimed that the troops of his competitor had followed that crook against their will; the leader who had lost was put to death and, "according to custom, his head was brought" to the winner. In politics, Rome had no other punishment than capital, as any opposition was considered treason. However, some believe that Zenobia was spared that fatal outcome.

The emperors were reduced to defending only the Danube front, which provided access to Italy and to Rome itself. And since they themselves were at the head of armies and no longer had lieutenants, they couldn't be everywhere at the same time. So those in the provinces had to improvise their own defense; more than one region or city tried to escape disaster by submitting to an ad hoc local leader, because every province wanted an emperor who was close to it. We'll soon see how this explains the Palmyrene saga.

For ten years Gaul, which had been destroyed by the raids of the *Germanii*, thus had a lineage of emperors for itself alone. This wasn't the revenge of Vercingetorix, but an emergency measure to save that bit of the Roman Empire; the "emperors of the Gauls" were patriots who worshipped eternal Rome in the captions on their coins. What is more, one of them proclaimed on his own coins that he was the "restorer of the entire Roman world," and that the Orient rightfully belonged to him. The empire was one and indivisible.

8

The Palmyrene Saga

In 251, benefitting from the misfortune of the times, Palmyra became a hereditary principality and vassal of Rome, under the rule of a family whose successive dynasts were Odaenathus and Wahballat (we'll come across these names again), who were given the title, invented for them, of "exarch of the Palmyrenes;" the magistrates of the city had preserved their functions under their authority. And so in Palmyra a great family had acquired primacy over others, something that often happened in many aristocratic cities. Two generations earlier, this family had received Roman citizenship, through a favor that was rarely granted in Palmyra. The one who was dynast in 251 had even been raised by Rome to the rank of Roman senator: he entered into that senatorial order, some thousand families strong, that formed the governing body of the entire empire. They each ensured loyalty to Rome.

The new exarch was essentially the de facto master of the entire Palmyrene region, its settled citizens, and its itinerant shepherds, all of whom would one day be his warriors. That a prince-like vassal could also be a senator wasn't new. That Rome would have vassal princes was even less so; let's remember Herod Antipas (the one who had John the Baptist's head cut off after Salome danced in front of him): his title of tetrarch of Galilee was no more unique than were those of exarch of Palmyra or phylarch of the Safaitic Arabs; these were titles of minor chiefs, not sovereigns. But there was a rule to be respected: a vassal received his crown from Rome; he didn't get it himself or from his predecessor.

Ten years later, the empire's situation became even worse and the unbelievable occurred: in 259 or 260, on the eastern front, the emperor Valerian himself was taken prisoner by the king of Persia, Sapor, King of Kings. "The situation in the East being desperate," wrote a Greek historian, "[Gallienus] ordered to come to its rescue Odaenathus of Palmyra, a man whose ancestry had been held in honor by the Emperors. This man, when he had mixed in as many of his own men as he could with the army that had been left there [those that hadn't gone to fight against Sapor], attacked Sapor in force."[13]

This Odaenathus was "the leader of the Saracens of the region of Palmyra," wrote a Byzantine historian (the term "Saracen" or Arab" was used for any group of people that lived in tents and led a nomadic life). He was a senator like his predecessor, and had even received the supreme title of Roman consul. Here was a vassal dynast, integrated into the governing class, who was capable of raising a private army made up of his own nomads and of standing up to a Persian raid; he must certainly have had an enormous fortune and a vast number of people to call upon.

The emperor, consumed by the war in the West, had to yield to necessity; he relied on some legal maneuvering, since, if we are to believe our author, he made Odaenathus responsible for the defense of the region. Odaenathus assembled his nomads and the auxiliaries that Rome had earlier raised among them and, leading the charge, in 261 he defeated Sapor on the Oronte River; an entire portion of desert was wrested from the King of Kings. The emperor was able to proclaim himself "great victor over the Persians" on his coins: he was the victor through the success of his Palmyrene lieutenant.

Those exploits were greatly admired, and with good reason: Persia, although always threatening, ceased to be a mortal danger for three centuries to come.

Odaenathus had become the most famous man of his time; he had inflicted a defeat on the Persians on the Oronte. However, the conflict had not entirely ended. Following their military custom, the Persians waged against the empire less of a war of conquest than one of annual incursions that were carried out in succession like so many raids, with the taking of populations that were brought back to Persia as living spoils for forced labor; Antioch was raided twice in six years. As is explained by our sources from that time, "on two occasions" Odaenathus arrived at the walls of the enemy's capital, the impregnable Ctesiphon, not far from Bagdad. Throughout six successive years, he fought more than one invasion and twice pursued the King of Kings, who was forced to flee. Syria was saved, and the Roman province of Mesopotamia, on the right banks of the Euphrates, was taken back from the Persians. Zenobia would soon take for her own use the foreign forces that terrified the Roman soldiers: the armored heavy cavalry, riders who carried lances and were covered in metal armor; they were called *cataphracts* or *clibanarii*—that is, "metallic furnace" in Persian—due to the armored riders becoming overheated.

Odaenathus had become the de facto true master of Syria and the province of Mesopotamia; he, and then Zenobia, his widow, would remain so until 272. As for the five legions of Syria, who were dedicated to a defense against Persia, they had clearly aligned themselves with the savior of the Roman Orient, because the day had arrived when Odaenathus was able to confront Sapor on an actual battlefield instead of simply pursuing him in retreat. Palmyra had recovered its security; in 266 caravan traffic had resumed. Odaenathus's hold over all of Syria was so solidly established that he dared to leave and to travel at a distance to defend the entire empire and repel other invaders, the Goths, who had become pirates and were ravaging the coasts of the Black Sea. On his way, in 267, he was assassinated on the initiative of one of those close to him who accused him of "preparing to upset the state" and to seize the imperial throne. The murderer thought he was serving the interests of the ruling emperor, who, in fact welcomed him warmly. In vain: upon Odaenathus's death, Zenobia inherited all the power that her husband had acquired.

Central power in Rome had thus been forced to allow Odaenathus free rein in Syria. In these years when the Roman Empire was ruling essentially in name only, each region lived its particular life, but there was no enemy of Roman imperialism that was able to benefit from its weakened position to overthrow it. When a population revolted, it was not out of nationalism, but against the weight of taxation.

Here is a positive fact: the one who beat Sapor had assembled his eastern possessions into a sort of kingdom while continuing to believe that he was still part of the empire. Nor did he attempt to usurp the imperial throne, or perhaps he didn't have time to do so. The necessary and sufficient proof of this is that there is no coinage in his name, whereas the first item of business of usurpers was to mint coins to pay their soldiers and to have their imperial title read by their subjects. Odaenathus remained loyal to his sovereign until his premature death. His widow wouldn't do the same; a second chapter in the saga was about to begin.

Zenobia had inherited the kingdom, the army, and those who were loyal to her husband; in an unregulated society without a real constitution, each individual invested his interests in the patronage of a powerful family; that family would protect its followers in order to preserve its own hereditary interests, and each individual would preserve his own interests by remaining attached to it; which explains loyalties that would last for generations and whose duration and apparent irrationality might surprise us. Zenobia took charge of her realm; the coin mints of Antioch and Alexandria, of which she soon became the mistress, created coins both in her name and in that of her son Wahballat, because Zenobia ruled as a queen. She established a city, which was the most significant gesture a sovereign power could make, and that she alone could do; and she gave it her name, as was the custom. She went on to conquer Egypt, and Arabia in passing, and to inscribe her name everywhere throughout her kingdom—on road markers of the Phoenician port of Byblos and on those of Bostra, the capital of the Roman province of Arabia.

Like a Hellenic queen, she surrounded herself with educated men. Callinicos, an Arab from Petra who occupied the public chair of rhetoric in Athens, dedicated a book to her in which he compares her to Cleopatra. The supreme leader had a duty to be in contact with all schools of thought; she had her own philosopher, the Platonist Cassius Longinus.

In addition to her taste for learning, Zenobia also had a religious sensibility. One of her contemporaries who frequented her court, Paul of Samosata, a Syrian bishop and great lord, wrote that Zenobia was attracted, perhaps even more than attracted, to Judaism,[14] which at the time was an avant-garde religion, and which practiced proselytism, attracting souls by its profound piety, its monotheism, and its demanding rituals. Great Roman ladies had synagogues built and, already two centuries earlier, a princess of the imperial house had become one of the sympathizers whom the Jews called "God-fearing." Zenobia also granted asylum to Manicheans. This second universal religion that had just been born (its prophet, Mani, would become a martyr in Persia five years later) once extended as far as China and lasted a thousand years. It has even been suggested, probably wrongly, that Languedocian Catharism arose out of it. We should point out that Zenobia, like Catherine II of Russia, had the interest, the capacity, and the ability to connect with the intelligentsia, who had influence over her governing decisions; by playing the immemorial card of the philhellene foreign sovereign she earned the friendship of the Greek provinces of the empire.

She was called a queen in Greek and in Aramaic, and "mother of the King of Kings," because her son Wahballat had assumed the glorious title of his father. Like Agrippina before her, she reigned under the shadow of her son, who was king to the outside world. In Antioch, the capital of Roman Syria, Wahballat had coins minted, as a sovereign would do; on his coins and in his inscriptions he announced his title as *rex* in Latin, the official language of central power, because he didn't want to oppose the Orient and Rome. Zenobia had thus settled the status of her domination in the interior.

But what about the exterior? What relationships could this sovereign maintain with a Rome where the emperor Aurelian was attempting to reconstruct the unity of the empire?

Then began five years (267–72) of a tragedy in three acts that ended with the catastrophe that would put an end to

Zenobia's reign, to the eastern "kingdom," and to the prosperity of Palmyra, whose grandeur would henceforth disappear from history: Two acts of great political maneuvering and probably diplomatic negotiations, followed by a military epilogue. Zenobia didn't undertake to break from Rome. On the contrary, she had two successive policies: she tried first to carve a place for herself in the empire, then, second, to take the reins from it.

The first act covered the three years before Aurelian's appearance. Zenobia, who set her sights high, proposed and tried to impose an original solution: that Wahballat be emperor in the Orient and Aurelian be emperor in the West, the emperor of the West all the same having a rank superior to that of his colleague.

For once, our documentation is conclusive: in public inscriptions, official documents, and monetary captions, words were law; to call oneself emperor was already to perform a coup d'état; to inscribe one's name on road markers was a royal privilege. On the road to Byblos, a marker pays homage both to the ruling sovereign, called "August," and to Wahballat, who is simply noted as "Emperor." Wahballat thus claimed to establish on his own a bicephalous regime in which two emperors, one of which was above the other, would reign together. It was an enormous project, but we are certain it was attempted.

Every Roman sovereign had the exclusivity of "Emperor," which in this case was a sort of first name, and that of "August," a "last name" that was even more weighty than the first. Here, the sovereign of Rome was August whereas Wahballat more modestly called himself only Emperor.

In 270, the coins minted in Alexandria following Zenobia's conquest of Egypt give proof of the unequal division of the empire. The busts of Aurelian and Wahballat are facing each other; both are wearing imperial insignia, breastplate and mantle. Under the bust of Aurelian one reads "August"; under that of Wahballat, "Emperor."

The division was a bold project, but not utopian: it followed the direction in which history seemed to be moving. Now that the reigning emperor had personally to be present everywhere, the multiplication of sovereigns appeared to many to be the only solution to the problems of the century: battles along the borders; the incessant *pronunciamientos* of governors and generals—that is, what might be called patriotic anarchy.

Twice already, in 244 and 253 and again in 276 following the fall of Palmyra, the reigning emperor had conferred the eastern provinces to one of his brothers, or to a worthy man whom he named "rector" or "duke" of the Orient. At the beginning of the century two brothers, Caracalla and Geta, reigned together; they had planned, it was claimed, to divide the empire between them: the elder would have the West and would establish his army in present-day Istanbul, the gateway to Europe; the younger would establish his realm in the opposite direction, on the other side of the Bosphorus, in Chalcedon, the gateway to Asia (let's remember the name of Chalcedon; we will come across it soon in dramatic circumstances); and so they both raised the guard on the passage between the two continents, and each could prevent the other from crossing the straits to launch an attack. This ingenious and somewhat childish tale shows that the idea of separating the East and the West wasn't new. Fifteen years after the fall of Zenobia, the great emperor Diocletian would indeed achieve, under other terms, this division between two sovereigns of unequal rank, a division of which Zenobia had sketched the early design. We can measure the weight of the Palmyrene episode in history when we remember that after

Zenobia the unity of the empire had finally come to an end, except for four or five short-lived episodes that would last less than thirty years.

The "queen" of Palmyra took an additional step forward following her easy conquest of Egypt in 270 at the head of an army "made up of Palmyrenes, Syrians, and Barbarians"; seizing the land of the Nile enabled her to hold Rome hostage by controlling the flow of food out of Egypt and raising its price, since the Roman plebs obtained their daily bread, a form of taxation, from Egypt. Henceforth, public acts were dated from the common reign of "our lords Aurelian and Wahballat, both August." This unilateral fait accompli was a proposal addressed to the emperor to share the empire; it was a foundation for negotiation. Aurelian refused or didn't respond. And so Zenobia decided to go for all or nothing: she marched on Rome.

It was not unheard of for a provincial or even Oriental family to take power in Rome. At the beginning of the century a great sovereign, Septimius Severus (the one who had made Odaenathus's grandfather a Roman citizen), was a Libyan of Phoenician origin who spoke Carthaginian with his own grandfather, just as Zenobia spoke Aramaic. Two generations before Zenobia, the city closest to Palmyra, Emesa, had already succeeded in what Palmyra was attempting: two princesses with strong personalities, who came from a dynasty of high priests that was the true master of the city, had become the wives and mothers of emperors and had installed a Syrian family on the imperial throne.

And only twenty years earlier, a military figure from the province of Arabia had ruled; he is known by the name Philip the Arab. He was a native of present-day Shahba, a museum city, in a land that at that time was Arabian, not Syrian, around a hundred kilometers south of Damascus. Having reached the highest ranks of the imperial hierarchy and crushed an offensive by the Persians, he was made emperor in February 244. He quickly left the Orient and, on July 23, entered Rome in solemn procession.

A quarter century after Philip the Arab, the Palmyrene army began to march and entered Anatolia, a part of the empire. But to expand her conquests was not Zenobia's true goal: she wanted everything, she wanted Rome, and she was ready to reconstruct the unity of the empire to her own benefit. What happened next is revelatory of her intentions, such as I modestly believe I understand them.[15] The Palmyrenes, wrote a Greek historian, "had seized the entire East as far as Ancyra; they also wanted to occupy Bithynia as far as Chalcedon," which today is a suburb of Istanbul located on the eastern banks of the Bosphorus. In my opinion, for an ancient reader, just the name of Chalcedon, known as the main entrance to Europe, said it all: the true goal of the expedition was not to conquer Anatolia but to cross the narrows to conquer the emperor in the West and solemnly proceed into Rome.

By leaving Syria, by invading Anatolia, Zenobia had thrown down the gauntlet. What would have been surprising, in my opinion, is if she hadn't: as we saw earlier, wars between pretenders to the imperial throne, each followed by their respective troops, the most adventurous coup d'états in two centuries, had woven the fabric of Roman history. Such was *normal* political life at that time, as close presidential elections are for us. Populations bore the brunt of this, but they knew that such was life.

To become master of Syria and Egypt, then go on to Europe and show one's imperial head to the people of the capital, Rome, and to the Roman Senate! This is what another usurper, named Macrian, had attempted ten years earlier (he was defeated and executed in western Turkey or in

Yugoslavia). Like Macrian, the Palmyrenes followed the great route, 1,100 kilometers long, that went from Syria to Chalcedon through Ancyra, present-day Ankara, by crossing all of eastern Turkey on a diagonal. Along the way there was only one legion to stop them; they probably obtained supplies by sacking cities and the countryside along the way. Once they had crossed the Bosphorus, another historic path opened up before them as it had before Macrian; from Constantinople/ Istanbul, the gateway to the West, it led to the valley of the Save, which travels through the former Yugoslavia.

To go to war in that empire was first to cover even more ground than Napoleon's soldiers had to do. The decisive battle would have taken place somewhere along that route. After their victory, the Palmyrenes would continue toward Trieste in Italy to march on Rome, because one couldn't be a successful sovereign without having a solemn procession into the capital to harangue the Senate and show oneself in the Circus to the Roman people, who were very sensitive on that point.

All the same, the reader might ask, was it possible that a Syrian woman could have become a Roman empress? Yes; for a good half-century Orientals, Phoenicians, and Arabs followed one another onto the imperial throne! And why did a new sovereign need to go to Rome to be seen? Because one didn't "feel" like an emperor and wasn't fully seen as one without the ratification of the senators.

As for the people of Rome, they had in no way become the apolitical plebs that the satirical poets of the time claimed, those who railed against the city's "decadence" as critics, many of them talented, always do. Roman citizens considered themselves masters of the world, and they were very punctilious about the respect they felt was owed them by the emperors in person; they expected or demanded to be visited by them.

For Zenobia and her son, the only conscious or implicit framework of thought and of political action, their "discourse," was the empire. Like an ideal, like a dream, that "discourse," after it had been erased through reality and actions, would live in memory until the century of Dante.

But Zenobia had the emperor Aurelian to contend with. Born near present-day Sofia or perhaps in Croatia—we don't know which—this son of peasants, an officer who came up from the ranks, was not an aristocrat in the old style, but one of those emperor-soldiers, the issue of Danubian and Balkan regions, who had saved the empire in the aforementioned tragic times. He battled the barbarians on the lower Danube, but anticipated the Palmyrenes' maneuver. Let's pause and spare a thought for the imperial couriers who, we might assume, came racing toward him to bring the news of the Palmyrene expedition, picking up fresh horses every thirty-five kilometers or so.

At the head of the fearsome and jealous Danubian army (because, as we know, armies were jealous of each other), Aurelian rode through Bulgaria right into Istanbul and the Bosphorus, passing into Asia, and his army marched to meet the Palmyrenes. He fought them out of Ancyra, Antioch, and Emesa, forcing them to turn around and seek refuge in Palmyra, and then became master of that city without much difficulty. Zenobia tried to escape to Persia but was taken prisoner.

By 272 Zenobia's imperial and dynastic dream had come to an end; it had lasted only two years. The victor had the philosopher Cassius Longinus put to death. The Manicheans had found refuge outside the empire, in Hira; they lived there with pagans, Jews, Zoroastrians, and Christians. From there, the Manichean religion reached the oases of the northwestern Arabian peninsula, controlled by dynasts who had converted to Judaism, and it finally reached Medina and Mecca. As for Aurelian, he undertook to reconquer Egypt and to quell the other rebellion that was mutilating the empire: that of the "Gallic emperors." He succeeded easily, after which Germanic raids started up again in full force. The integrity of the empire was maintained for another dozen years. In 274 in Rome, Aurelian celebrated his triumph over Palmyra and Gaul. He was assassinated the following year; we don't know why.

What about Zenobia and Wahballat? We don't know how or when Wahballat died. As for what became of his mother, ancient historians have provided three different versions. The one fact that is fairly certain is that she was captured, and that Aurelian paraded his prisoner in front of the people in the capital of Syria. But what then? According to a very uninformed chronicler, she was dragged in the triumphal procession, then decapitated, following the Roman practice of putting the enemy leader to death on the evening of the procession (this is how Vercingetorix ended up). According to another historian, Zenobia died of an illness or starved herself to death on a boat that was bringing her to Rome to be displayed; that version, as prosaic as reality, neither foreseeable nor romantic, seems most plausible to me.

Then there is the exciting version: Zenobia, paraded through the streets but in chains of gold, and then pardoned, settled in Tivoli in a gilded retreat, took a senator as her second husband, and had one of her daughters marry . . . Aurelian. This happy ending can be read in a serious book, the *Histoire Auguste*, in which true events, some Alexandre Dumas, fairy tales, and a bit of *Ubu Roi* (in the biography of Heliogabalus) all come together.

The same author painted an irresistible portrait of Zenobia, with her black eyes and her sense of defiance. Following

the exploits of Odaenathus, the saga of a woman had established the place of the "queen" of Palmyra in the gallery of
illustrious men. Ancient authors compare her to Cleopatra,
but, in contrast to the queen of Egypt, attribute chastity to
her; they saw in her all the virile and feminine virtues, and
Arab geographers would make her a figure of legend.

No one knew anything about what she really looked like.
We have coins of Zenobia on which her profile appears, but we
can't rely on monetary portraits. Let's remember Cleopatra's
nose: on half her coinage the lover of Caesar and Antony has
the pure profile and nose of a Greek goddess; on the other
half she has the nose of an eagle and the aquiline chin that
engravers gave to heads of state. And those are the nose and
chin that Zenobia has on her own coins: an imperial profile.

9

A Hybrid Identity

Zenobia had the dual identity of an Oriental queen (like Queen Berenice in Caesarea, who had a love affair with Titus) and a true Roman citizen. She broke with the empire, only to come immediately under the protection of another power, that of Persia, whose culture was not her own and where she herself was nothing. In antiquity there wasn't the modern notion of the nation, a coming together of ethnicity and the state; political formations at that time were easily multiethnic. Nor did antiquity recognize a plurality of independent states: independence belonged only to nomadic or mountain-dwelling tribes; it was found in the isolation of small barbarian groups. Independence was relative and wasn't a matter of all or nothing. Above all, the reality of the empire, the necessity of Roman domination for the local elite, was ubiquitous.

The empire was the social order of those times. In every corner of its domain, Rome with its legions provided and assured the wealthy and powerful in each location the most important commodity of all: the preservation of their power. It turned them into "collaborators." This is how the Roman Empire continued to survive—not through its good laws, or because the Romans might have had a sense of organization more effective than that of their neighbors; they were convinced that they had been born to rule over the entire world.

Wealth, power, Persia, Greece, Rome and its emperors: all these components of that time are gathered in a carving on a sarcophagus discovered in Palmyra. The cover of this stone coffin is carved in the shape of a banquet bed, following a Greco-Roman motif. However, the deceased carved on the bed is wearing a magnificently embroidered Persian garment whose parallel folds are typical of an archaic Middle-Eastern style.

The chest of the sarcophagus is decorated in bas-relief with a scene of a religious nature: we see the same deceased person performing a sacrifice. This talented work and the Greco-Roman style unite all the deceased's various roles. He is wearing a wide headpiece with a frontal medallion, the insignia of priests in both Palmyra and throughout the empire; thus he was a priest, fairly common among Palmyrene notables. But he has exchanged his Oriental garment for a toga, a very unusual ceremonial garment in Palmyra which only Roman citizens had the right to wear; thus he was one of the rare notables in that city who had been granted Roman citizenship.

At his sides two men, wearing the short tunic of common citizens, respectively carry a fowl and a platter of fruit. We are well acquainted with these figures: from la Moselle to Tunisia and Egypt, funerary reliefs, mosaics, and paintings show the procession of peasants who, once every year, solemnly bring to their master the harvest of his lands: a basket of fruit, a hare, a rooster. These were timeless, obligatory gifts symbolizing the link of dependency; they were also sacrificial gifts to the gods to thank them for the harvest of the past year. Our deceased Palmyrene, proud of his Roman citizenship, is represented as a great landowner who ruled over his peasants.

We might therefore speak of a patriotism for the empire, which by definition was foreign to these "ethnic" identities that are well known today, as well as to a sense of national past.

And yet that past was not truly forgotten: in Roman Tunisia a polythematic writer, Apuleius, steeped to the tips of his fingers in Greco-Roman culture, was proud of his Carthaginian origins; another native Carthaginian who spoke the language, the emperor Septimius Severus, an imperial patriot if ever there was one, had Hannibal's tomb restored. Appian, a Greek from Egypt who wrote the history of Rome as a true Roman, in his preface sings the praises of his rulers of the past, pharaohs and Greek kings; and the Gallic nobility took names ending in "–rix" to establish the ancientness of their origins.

The empire encompassed all the local pasts; the empire was "us" against the "others." One mustn't interpret the Oriental garment that men wore in Palmyra as being a symbol of competition with the Greek mantle. Elsewhere in the empire, noblewomen had sculptures of themselves depicted in their national costumes created for their funerary stelae: long flowing sleeves in Belgium; a tall, conical headpiece wrapped with a veil in Carinthia and Slovenia; a turban in Tyrol; a fur hat whose wide brims formed two horns in Hungary. These were manifestations of identity, not symbols of separatist intent.

After the fall of Zenobia and the capture of the city, Palmyra disappeared from history. The city was sacked by Aurelian,[16] but it wasn't destroyed. The following century, the Christian fourth century, wasn't at all a "low empire," the era of the "decadence of Rome," in spite of a tenacious legend. But Palmyra would be absent from it; far from losing its population, it saw the construction of four churches and had a bishop, but it was henceforth only a city-fortress to defend against Persia. The city's final appearance on the historical public stage took place in the time when Charlemagne's son was ruling in France: the caliph of Bagdad had his scholars measure a meridian arc between Palmyra and the Euphrates, and the results were remarkably accurate.

It is still difficult to determine which ethnicity Palmyra might have claimed as its own. Was it an Aramean city? Arab? This is a question that continues to be debated passionately even now. Were the escapades of Odaenathus and Zenobia the Arab saga that some claim? But, for ancient writers, "Arab" often simply meant "nomad." The other daughter of the desert, Petra, had an Arab population, in the ethnic sense of the term, but those Arabs had adopted Aramaic as their written language while keeping Arabic as the liturgical language of their polytheism; Greek inscriptions there are rare. In Palmyra the foundation was Aramean, but the Arab component ended up taking over through sheer numbers. So we have an ancient Aramean city in which Arabs came to settle and whose language they adopted; their divinities got along well with those of the Palmyrenes. We can see then how Arabs penetrated into Syria before Islam, and also how they were "Arameanized."

It would be important to know whether the heroes of the Palmyrene saga considered themselves Orientals or members of the imperial elite. The answer is clear. The common people did not understand Greek; they spoke Aramaic, and continued to speak it for a long time. Aristocrats spoke it at home, but the language that befit their status was not at such a provincial level; they belonged to the international elite, which was Hellenized everywhere. Their children learned Greek through Aesop's *Fables* (the notebook, or rather the tablets, of a student who copied the *Fables* have been found in Palmyra), and they bore official imperial titles. They belonged to the exclusive club of the masters of the world.

Zenobia, herself, as a woman, had even more reason to think that way. It was in Hellenism, in the civilization of Queen Cleopatra and the powerful Roman princesses, that "Queen" Zenobia could find a role suitable to her stature.

The history of Palmyra would have been that of a small society that lived on the edges of a great civilization, one that the members of its elite more or less took as their own, leading to a mixed culture. Palmyra holds the record for the number of rich cultures that could be found in one place. One need only observe a map of the empire; there isn't any other region where one might have encountered a greater number of influences: ancient Mesopotamia, ancient Aramean Syria, Phoenicia, some of Persia, more of Arabia, and covering it all was Greek culture and the Roman political framework. "Cultural chauvinism, the invention of the nineteenth century," writes Ernest Will, "was unknown in antiquity."[17]

All of this made Palmyra a patchwork city. Palmyrene funerary portraits were divided just about evenly between priests with their heads and cheeks shaven, wearing headpieces and holding sacred branches, libation vessels, or incense boxes in their hands, and men with nothing on their heads who are holding books or writing tablets. Holding books! In Hellenistic art and throughout the Roman Empire deceased nobles are not represented with a sword at their side. It was culture that distinguished a person; books and tablets showed that the deceased belonged to the elite, that he had led a life of leisure, and that he had engaged in liberal studies.

Priests, however, came out of the same milieus as other notables, and had received the same education. Their priesthood, or function as heads of the sacred banquet, was as much a social status as it was a religious mission; in fact, what seems to have distinguished priests and the educated are the two partial interpretations that Palmyrenes might have had of their own society, the first more traditional and local, the second more international. It depended on each individual's taste; to prefer the Persian garment or the Greek mantle was a matter of personal choice, of wealth, or of whim, not of origin nor of profession.

A patchwork city to be sure, but in its own way: Palmyra was different from any other city in the empire; it and Edessa were the only cities where the Oriental dialect remained an official language. The architectural elements of the city are Greek overall, though perhaps not in the details; the ambition and culture of the elite were those of the rest of the empire, as were the embellishments of their lives; but in religion, in the art of the local sculptors, and in collective diversions, there was a profound transformation of appearances and preservation of their way of thinking. Palmyra had been a daughter of the desert far too long to change completely.

Some Greco-Roman customs were introduced, however, including that of the public baths (which became the hammams, and which represented one of the pleasures of life rather than a concern with hygiene). In the second century Palmyra had one of those profane baths, which was different from those that were installed in sanctuaries to purify pilgrims. A bilingual inscription celebrates a wealthy individual who, in the year he was secretary of the city, had provided free oil (which was used as soap) for all those who used the public baths, both foreigners and citizens. This must have been quite costly, because in that year the emperor Hadrian, a great traveler, had come to stay in Palmyra along with his civil and military escort. In exchange, the man's fellow citizens honored him with a statue and that inscription. It has also been noted that, beyond any civic function, the magnates of Palmyra came to the aid of caravans in trouble: a sheik had a duty to be generous and to help those of his tribe in need.

So, were these wealthy citizens or sheiks? Was it civic patronage, or tribalism? Greece or the old Orient? In any preindustrial society there was nothing more common than for the powerful to show proof of their generosity; it was the virtue of lords and kings, whose bounty extended from on high to their inferiors. What is surprising is the coexistence of taxation and charity; seigneurial generosity subsisted within the civil system. We might have assumed a priori that, as in our time, all citizens were equal after having been institutionally measured, and that the wealth of a citizen was taken into consideration only at the time of calculating to the very penny the amount his taxes should be. Indeed, here we have what wasn't said, the "discourse," that separated the ancient world from ours.

Unlike the modern citizen, the ancient citizen was not an abstract figure. If he was rich and powerful as an individual, he remained so as a citizen. He thus had the right to offer his city oil for the baths, to build a theater for it, to join his warriors to come to the aid of a caravan, or, like the future emperor Augustus, to use his financial resources to assemble a private army to liberate the republic that was being threatened by a faction. In Palmyra, the Aramean or Arab magnates could thus without contradiction be generous in two different roles: that of the head of a clan and that of a patriotic citizen.

The city had adopted certain Greek customs while ignoring others, of which it perhaps had indigenous equivalents. Palmyra had only one public bath (whereas little Lutèce, now Paris, had three) and seems to have foregone circus races and gladiator battles, which were much less popular in Syria than in the Latin West and the Greek Orient. Something even more curious: Palmyra did not adopt a decisive component of Hellenism—athletic competitions, which we call "games," as in Olympic "games." These athletic or theatrical competitions had always been of great importance in the life of a Hellenic city, a great moment of the year. There weren't competitions in Petra or Emesa, either, both of which were Arab cities, whereas the rest of Syria enjoyed many such games.

And yet a small theater was discovered in Palmyra (figure 8), one that could have scarcely held one or two thousand spectators, because it has only twelve rows of seats, forming a single level. There were no theatrical competitions in Palmyra. Without regular competitions, performances must have been given only occasionally, when a patron offered one to his fellow citizens, for example, and paid for a troupe to be brought in.

What sort of performances were they? We can only guess. There were probably "mimes" and "pantomimes," stage genres that didn't enter into the realm of competitions; nor did actors wear masks in them. Pantomime was a unique mixture of music, song, and dance in which a mute dancer mimed on stage the attitudes and gestures of his role while corresponding melodies were sung in the wings by another actor; female roles were played by men. Mime was a comedy, either high or lowbrow, fantastic or slapstick, in which women did have roles; it could also be a "remake" of a well-known play. The language used was certainly Greek. This genre was very popular, and a mime was often staged to celebrate imperial accessions. In the end, Syrians, for whom theater was a foreign novelty, became interested in it; the great number of theater structures attest to this.

The theater of Palmyra, one of the smallest in the ancient world, might also have been used for religious representations, such as those that appeared in the cults of Syria (sanctuaries sometimes included small, simple installations for this purpose); we can imagine that on feast days a costumed actor onstage sang a hymn to Attis accompanied by a cithara, or that a female singer celebrated the annual return of Adonis.

But today, Palmyra's theater has been used for filmed "performances" that are quite different. This theater has been used to stage horrible and ostentatious executions, mass slaughters undertaken by the terrorist organization ISIS. For example, on July 4, 2015, twenty-five Syrian soldiers were lined up side-by-side, kneeling in front of the colonnade at the back of the theater, as seen in a widely disseminated photo. Behind each kneeling man stood one of the twenty-five executioners, holding a weapon; in an instant those men's throats would be cut, or their heads cut off.

As for the archeological museum of Palmyra, today it has been used as a tribunal and prison.

10

Dining with the Gods

What was of greatest importance to Palmyrenes was not performances or competitions, but a uniquely Oriental custom: sacred banquets in which a god participated, becoming part of his adorers' celebrations. These were hosted by the priests of the great temples and by a group of confraternities, called *marzeah* in both Palmyrene and Hebrew, each of which gathered a handful of members and worshipped a divinity they had chosen—Allat, for example, or Bel and Allat, or Allat and Malakbel—using the dues that each member paid. More than fifty gods have been counted, often associated patriotically with Bel, the great god of the city. Most important was that each *marzeah* invited many guests to its annual feast. A large percentage of the population benefited from this hospitality, as we know through terra cotta tesserae that were used as invitation chits; a large number of these have been found, and thirteen hundred different types have been identified. During the feast, an animal victim was sacrificed to the god of the confraternity and eaten by the guests, who were stretched out on banquet beds; the god was believed to occupy one of the beds, opposite the revelers.

The banquet and its utensils (craters, ladles, jugs, wine containers with their contents inscribed) are represented on the tesserae: the priests of the confraternities, wearing their headpieces, are lying on banquet beds, cups in their hands, served by a cup bearer; or they are busy doling out portions of meat, bread, and wine for their guests; we can see the accounting, read the quantities. The sacrificial animals were sheep or camels, both of which would be eaten. Finally, we see the presence of the god himself, that of his banquet bed which is empty of any visible figure or effigy. Under the image, an inscription gives the name of the god or that of the confraternity ("religious society of the priests of Bel," "confraternity of Nebo") or even that of its president, called head of the banquet. It is significant that these inscriptions are in Aramaic, not Greek.

These feasts were offered by a sanctuary, a tribe, a clan, or just individuals. The priests of the great Temple of Bel, in addition to their sacred function, formed a confraternity that sent invitations, and their high priest also bore the title, in Greek, of head of the banquet. A pious donor gave a perpetual banquet donation: he paid the priests of Bel the amount of four hundred coins, the interest on which enabled them to "distribute meat to all those who, on August 16 of each year, will be invited to eat in the presence of the god Manno."

Here we see what separated two forms of religion and what perhaps united two forms of mundanity. In Greece, too, every sacrifice was followed by a banquet where the faithful consumed the meat of the victim, leaving the god only the bones and smoke; in Greece, too, the less religious souls above all saw in a sacrifice the banquet that would follow. The difference is that during the banquet, the Greeks celebrated only amongst themselves: they were not eating along with the god; mortals and the powerful foreign race of the gods maintained their distance. If a god were to come visit a Greek city, the city would install him in effigy on a bed and serve him a meal, as in Palmyra, but no one would sit at the table with the visitor. However, in Palmyra, in Egypt, in the Orient, a confident

familiarity brought together around the same table the patriarchal gods and their loving and devoted subjects.

That's all well and good, but let's not lose sight of the overall mundanity: were these feasts gatherings that were made
fervently religious by the invisible presence of a god, or were
they joyful parties where one ate meat, something which
many guests perhaps did only on such occasions, once or
twice a year? Can we believe in an entire population of devo-
tees, to a mass religious intensity?

Whatever the truth, it was an original component of the
cult of the gods. By contrast, if we look at the cult of the dead,
the ideas the Palmyrenes had about the beyond were not at all
unusual, had nothing Oriental about them, and were no loftier
than those of the rest of the empire. We can only judge from
the images that decorate their tombs, and they are borrowed
from Greece; they are scenes of so-called funereal banquets
that are found throughout the empire, and whose epitaphs
tell us that they depict the deceased as he was when he feasted
during his life. In Palmyra, as everywhere else, the deceased is
seen on his banquet bed, a drinking vessel in his hand, while
his wife is seated in a manner appropriate to the modesty of
her gender and is not drinking anything. These banquets are
not situated in the hereafter, but are tableaux of the life of
extreme leisure that the wealthy deceased once lived, family
meals where the living are next to the dead person. The banquet scene depicts both a family meal and a funerary banquet
celebrated every year in memory of the deceased.

For we have always managed to comfort ourselves with
ambiguous consolation. The ancients placed food on their
tombs; was it proof that they believed the dead somehow
continued to live within their tombs? When we place flow-
ers on a grave, do we believe that the deceased will arise to
enjoy their fragrant presence?

11

Religion in Palmyra

Syria, like Egypt, was a land of fervent religiosity whose ex-
uberant manifestations fascinated or scandalized the rest of
the empire. But there was something that is perhaps surprising to us: the pagan beliefs relating to the afterlife did not belong to religion, strictly speaking; the cult of the gods and the
cult of the dead were two distinct things.

Syrian exuberance must have existed in Palmyra: haunting
music, priests who slashed their arms or castrated themselves,
transvestites, sacred courtesans. . . . But our documentation
from Palmyra, while abundant, does not mention this. Rather,
it tells of a rich pantheon, with wonderful remains of a very
ancient mythology, very "modern" theological speculations,
of how the Syrian gods and those of the dominant Greek religion could be placed on the same level.

In paganism, very different gods coexisted peacefully. We
know of some sixty different divinities from Palmyra: gods
of tribes, the local god (Bel) who ruled over the city, foreign
divinities such as Isis. . . . They were not rivals. The most honored were Bel and Baalshamin, the "Lord of Heaven," the
god of storms and rain, dear to the farmers and herdsmen
throughout Syria. An ex-voto, today in a museum in Lyon,
shows the two gods side by side, and it goes without saying

that in Palmyra there was a lovely temple of Baalshamin, with four columns in the front.

But why, in August 2015, did ISIS need to blow up and destroy that temple of Baalshamin? Because it was a temple where pagans before Islam came to adore mendacious idols? No, it was because that monument was venerated by contemporary Westerners, whose culture includes an educated love for "historical monuments" and a great curiosity for the beliefs of other people and other times.[18] And Islamists want to show that Muslims have a culture that is different from ours, a culture that is unique to them. They blew up that temple in Palmyra and have pillaged several archeological sites in the Near East to show that they are different from us and that they don't respect what Western culture admires.

It is not envy, or jealousy of the superiority of the foreigner (as Anglophobia and Americanophobia have been in France), but the desire to prove and to prove to themselves that they are not like us, that they are themselves. Because really, what use is that destruction, not to mention all the attacks and massacres, to them, politically, tactically? To break with us, to show that they are different. They feel that their identity is misunderstood, whereas they alone have the true religion, the true customs, and have been gradually isolated in the wider world. Because Western culture and its customs extend over the entire globe, and even huge "Communist" China continues to be Westernized. Everywhere in the world, girls go to school, women drive. And for Westerners, if one of those admirable mosques in Damascus, Istanbul, or Adrianople were to be destroyed, it would be a tragic loss for all humanity.

Let's return to our ancient gods. There were many temples in Palmyra, because each tribe had brought its divinity there and every faithful individual could adore the god he had chosen; as a Palmyrene an Arab erected an altar to one of his gods "who doesn't drink wine" (probably the worshipper didn't drink wine, either). The warrior divinity of the Arabs, Allat, had a temple there where no sacrificial blood ever flowed. The Beni Mattabol were an Arab tribe from that region who nonetheless venerated Bel, as their name indicates. Bel or Bol, "the Lord," god of the great sanctuary, belonged to no tribe and floated above any tribal divisions. He can be seen as a sample of what a religion was in those times; we will see how in Palmyra, "scientific" astrological speculations came to modernize a mythical image of which the Bible itself has retained traces.

In archaic Syria, and then in Babylon, the Lord Bel had been the hero of a great myth: the confrontation of the god and the sea. Twenty centuries later, in Palmyra, a bas-relief in the Temple of Bel again represents him battling a monster with snakes for legs. This is the illustration of an ancient Mesopotamian poem, the text of which has been found on clay tablets and which tells of the creation of the world.

Everything unfolds as in Genesis, which was inspired by it: in the beginning all was but an aquatic chaos, everything was shapeless and covered by the sea, by Tiamat, the mother of all things, including the gods. It was one of them, Marduk, our Bel, who was able to vanquish Tiamat and push back the waters; she unleashed dragon-storms and snakes "with sharp teeth, pitiless jaws" against him, but in vain. After his victory, Marduk, having become the king of the gods, created humans to become his servants. In the Near East, a god often began by eliminating the chaos of the sea. In the Hebrew Bible, Yahweh, despite his incontestable originality, still conserves some poetic traces of the god who conquered monsters. "Thou didst divide the sea by thy strength: thou brakest the heads of the dragons in the waters. Thou brakest the heads of leviathan in pieces," says Psalms 74:13–14.

In Palmyra at the beginning of the Christian era, in the same temple where we saw the mythical battle between the god and the monster, an *aggiornamento* had conferred upon Bel a completely new and more exalted identity: that of an all-powerful god, lord of the astronomical heavens, identified with the Greek Zeus, king of the gods, of which the planet Jupiter was the symbol. On the temple ceiling the bust of Bel, or rather of his planet, is surrounded by the circle of the zodiac and the busts of the six other planets. As Henri Seyrig has shown,[19] that *aggiornamento* comes from the religion of educated men more than from the astrological tradition of Babylon. Far from representing a "primitive" adoration of the forces of nature, Bel's planetary aspect is a sign of modernity. Bel was not a solar god, but a cosmic one. This was an educated, astronomical speculation; it was Hellenistic.

Bel seated in his temple was not the only god to have had a cult; two other gods, unknown outside Palmyra, were associated with and subordinate to him, and were perhaps only aspects of that great god: Yarhibol, whose name seems to signify "moon of Bol," and Aglibol, who was the "calf of Bol" (bovine representations of the divinity had been common in the Orient, whence the Golden Calf mentioned in the Bible). The three divinities formed a trinity; on representations of them the two secondary gods surround Bel, one on his right, the other on his left. Aglibol is wearing a disc of the moon on his head, and Yarhibol, in spite of his name, wears the solar disc. Not that one was the god of the sun and the other that of the moon: here they are playing useful roles; they serve as bearers of the double astral symbol that meant "forever!" Everywhere in the empire the moon and the sun, or the allegories of dusk and dawn, surrounded beings who were promised eternity.

We must imagine that in Palmyra there was an educated, reasoning segment of society that was concerned with providing an acceptable interpretation of the gods to the other educated faithful; anthropomorphism was no longer enough. If we are surprised that the clergy in an oasis could have been aware of new ideas, we need only remember Apollonius of Tyana in the first century CE. At that time, that wise man, that theosophist who was venerated as a "divine man," traveled through Asia and Greece, and his influence reached as far as Syria. Along the way he preached, performed miracles, and visited sanctuaries to study them and to criticize the rituals, which he then had reformed by the local clergy. I am not suggesting that another Apollonius passed through Palmyra—only that ideas circulated freely.

Another anecdote may illustrate the primary theological issue of the time. A Syrian who went to live in Vaison (in present-day France), where he must have been successful in business, thanked Bel, whose oracle he had consulted before he left. The god had instructed his follower through oracles or dreams and prevented fortune from proving them wrong. Such was the great debate of those times, in which one was led to think abstractly and to see many divine figures as abstractions: Was the world dominated by blind fate, by unpredictable fortune, or by providential gods? In those times to be a nonbeliever, to be an independent thinker, did not amount to being an atheist, but meant one believed there was nothing to expect from the gods, and to no longer have anything to do with them. And so the triumph of a divinity was to win out over those other powers; this happened for Isis, that Egyptian Madonna who became popular throughout the empire. Litanies in her honor praise her for "*conquering* Destiny and making it obey."

Following the fall of Zenobia under the blows of Aurelian,

there was a great deal of talk even in Rome of an invincible supreme god, and opinion in Rome accused Bel of Palmyra of playing a role in that. Palmyra's long history shows what polytheism was at the time when Christianity began to spread. For a long time, high civilization and the moral authority of the empire and its ruler demanded that the state publicly honor a god of incontestable superiority who responded to the highest demands of the modern spirit. Not that a "natural" leaning toward monotheism existed at that time (nor perhaps at any other); to believe that the unifiers of the empire called upon monotheism through blind necessity is an old sociological supposition.

The times merely called for there to be not a single god, but an additional god, a god for everyone, whom all the subjects of the empire could adore alongside their national or personal gods. The sun was able to be that god for everyone: the indubitable and benevolent star, visible to the point of blinding, the emperor of the sky. It didn't have a mythological biography and was not anthropomorphic, it didn't even have a name the way humans did: it was what it was, the sun, a god that was both material and metaphysical. It would be a bit summary to see this new god as only an "ideology," a celestial copy of the person of the emperor, a bit of political propaganda. An astral religion suited the intellectual status of supreme power through its physical presence, one that was far superior to any revelation (and thus to Christian superstitions).

In Rome the sun already had worshippers and private cults. An educated prince, Gallienus, took a step in that direction and found the right adjective, which had two meanings; he minted coins with the effigy of a divine personification, *Sol invictus*, the "Unconquered Sun." Aurelian joined him in 274, on December 25, to consecrate his double victory over Palmyra and the Gauls. On that day of the winter solstice according to the Julian calendar, and of the birthday of the sun, he established a public cult of the Unconquered Sun (which meant that this cult would be celebrated by the state, and not imposed as a state religion). He built a temple to the sun in Rome, which no longer exists today.

But such religions of intellectuals and politicians left the ancient masses indifferent. Dozens of ex-votos have been found in Palmyra. In the large number of religious inscriptions, one finds no trace of what preoccupied the religious elite of the intelligentsia. The religious phenomenon wouldn't occupy such a large place in history if it was explained as a response to a fear of death or to a metaphysical enigma. Like the Greco-Roman masses, the Syrian masses expected from their gods protection, good harvests, and the procurement of worldly goods. They liked social occasions with a veneer of piety, and seasonal feasts that were warmer if they were religious. That materialism, if we may call it such, did not exclude a warm attachment to a good godly master—quite the opposite.

"We love the gods as we do our mothers and fathers," wrote Aristotle in book 9 of *Nicomachean Ethics*, and this was true of all paganism. People in the Orient reiterated their love for a deity. And in Palmyra more than elsewhere, a god was repeatedly told that he was good, merciful, had pity. Those were not effusions: the worshipper was alluding to precise circumstances wherein the divinity, granting the person's wishes, proved that he was compassionate. That love, then, was based on self-interest, which isn't contradictory.

That mundane paganism is the foundation of almost all religions; it hardly distinguished Syria from the rest of the empire. There was, however, a difference between Syrian religiosity and the civic pride of Greco-Roman paganism, just as there can be between two Christian denominations: one did not ask for material protection from a Syrian god and from a Greco-Roman god in the same way. Palmyrenes had a more patriarchal, more sentimental, less civic relationship with their pantheon than did the Greeks.

Palmyrenes' given names imply that they were slaves of a god; they were called, for example, Abdel, "servant of the god." Never would a Greek or a Roman worthy of those names have called himself a slave, even of a divinity; he would rather have died. Palmyrenes loved a patriarchal god, a celestial tribal chief who, for his part, loved his people; but in Greece the friendship and favoritism of a divinity for an individual was a brilliant exception that existed only in fiction (Athena loved Ulysses in the epic, and Artemis loved Hippolyta in the tragedy). In the Orient, the loving relationship was so reciprocal that a Palmyrene spoke of the piety that his gods showed toward him; one called piety a respect for divine and human laws vis-à-vis everyone. The gods of Palmyra respected the law that stated that a superior protected his own.

Aramean, Mesopotamian, Arab, and even Persian or Egyptian gods . . . they all came to Palmyra, where they were universally welcomed. The Palmyrenes weren't very particular about the origins of their ancestral gods; the offspring of an old native family counted the Egyptian Isis among them. But there was an exception: Palmyra didn't import any Greek or Roman divinities. Greek gods were present in Palmyra, but not through importation; they were present through translation. When Palmyrenes wrote in Greek, they rendered the name of their God Bel as "Zeus." This proves two things: that they saw themselves from the exterior with Greco-Roman eyes, and wanted to be understood by the rest of the empire; and that they admitted, along with all of non-Christian antiquity, that the gods of other peoples existed.

The Palmyrenes were well aware that, under their Aramean names, their gods were unknown in the wider world of which they considered themselves a part. They often wrote their ex-votos in Greek and it happened that they would transcribe verbatim, in Greek characters, the Aramean name of the god being honored, instead of substituting it with the name of the corresponding Greek god. The name of Bel was sometimes transcribed in Greek characters, and sometimes translated as "Zeus," because it went without saying that the Bel of Palmyra was none other than the Greeks' god known by the name of Zeus.

In Palmyra, Bel and Baalshamin, the gods of the heavens, were both translated by the one name Zeus. By contrast, Allat, the virgin warrior goddess, had two translations: the virgin Artemis or the warrior Athena. She had the face, the garb, and the weapons of the Greek Athena. There were plans to endow a new temple of Allat with an idol that was more beautiful than the images carved by the local artisans, and it was ordered from the renowned workshop of some great city; it was no doubt necessary to explain to the artist who Allat was, and it seemed to him that the goddess known by that name could only be Athena. Palmyra thus received a careful copy of the Athena holding her lance, or a work close to it, that Phidias had raised five hundred years earlier on the Acropolis of Athens. If a Greek person passing through Palmyra visited the temple of Allat, upon seeing the statue he might have concluded: "The divinity of this temple is Athena, because her image is that of the goddess."

12

Palmyrene Portraits

The Athena/Allat inspired by the work of Phidias is purely classical; it is a work of quality and a piece that was imported. The mosaic in the house of Cassiopeia (figure 11), which we mentioned earlier, also came from foreign hands to Palmyra, as did the stuccoes of mythological subjects in the Hellenistic style that decorate a private home (decorative elements of this type were generally the work of itinerant teams of artisans). We can suggest in principle that in Palmyra that which is Greco-Roman is the work of foreign artists, and that which is Oriental or a hybrid is the work of local artisans—or even that the public and private architecture is Hellenistic, then Greco-Roman, at least in its style, whereas the religious and funerary sculpture blends the Orient and the West, which gives it the unique character that we admire. I am referring to the famous "Palmyrene portraits," those busts of the dead that have done a great deal for the reputation of that ancient Oriental city (figure 9).

The Palmyrene portraits come from the tombs of wealthy families, where they were lined up by the dozens, on several superimposed rows. We know of more than a thousand, which clandestine digs and the trade in antiquities have dispersed from Damascus to Istanbul and Tokyo (all the great museums have attempted to acquire them). Those men with rich embroidered clothing, those women with heavy jewelry, excite our curiosity and reveal a whole spectrum of the past, satisfying a taste for the rare, the picturesque, a unique flavor, different values, and historical nostalgia, rather than for aesthetic beauty.

We dream of that mass of unknown men and women who have come to us one by one from a vanished era, with their faces, their clothing, and their jewelry: we know how fascinating faces and portraits can be. Time has unfortunately erased the colors that enhanced the realistic effects—because these busts were embellished with paint. Up to the time of Donatello, all ancient and medieval sculpture, reliefs and encrusted enamel, was covered in color; the Venus de Milo was blond and wore a blue mantle. On a Palmyrene portrait in the Louvre, the blue of a woman's eyes has endured to the present time.

We have just used the word "portrait," but those funerary images were not strictly meant to recall the traits of the deceased; they only vaguely resembled the person and weren't intended to do so; they symbolized the deceased more than they reproduced their traits: it was a man, a woman, a child, that's all.

Two images of the same woman, 'Ala, daughter of Yarhai, have been found in Palmyra; on one of them the deceased has a wide, square face; on the other, a narrow, triangular face; and on both, traits that are so nonindividualized that they cannot resemble anyone. On others, two Palmyrenes appear to resemble each other because their images must have come out of the same workshop. The artisan simply reduced faces to a series of formulas, and combined traits such as can be found on an identity card ("straight nose; average forehead; round face"), without having the talent or the desire to capture the individuality of the person, or to give an illusion of it.

His cursory carvings of average quality showed no anatomical precision or aesthetic imperative, and must not have been representative. The artisan was simply following the canons of beauty, placing a half-smile (sometimes prettily dissymmetrical) on the lips, and respecting the canons of the status of his subject, which differed depending on the gender: stiffness of men who raised their chin, a pouting mouth which revealed the chin in women. They don't have the unostentatious ease, the tranquil self-assurance of Greco-Roman portraits.

Before we leave Palmyra, let's go to the Louvre, where we find two large cases filled with Palmyrene busts. On first glance we note that they are realistic (or, using the technical term, naturalistic) effigies and artisanal productions, as can be seen in any archeological museum from Scotland to the Anatolian plateau, including Arlon, Narbonne, or Smyrna. In every large city of the empire and sometimes in small towns, the demand for portraits of the dead, for scenes of a "funerary banquet," or for ex-votos was satisfied by a local workshop that had its own style, or at least its own habits in regards to iconography and style.

All the same, in Palmyra, that local originality is more pronounced than elsewhere; busts and banquet scenes reveal an artistic originality that didn't correspond to the picturesque nature of the Oriental clothing. Their style, strictly speaking, is not Oriental; it is that of the Greco-Roman portrait throughout the empire. Despite a sometimes simplistic treatment, these effigies are less fixed, less stiff than might be expected; the faces appear individualized and the physiognomies are expressed in different ways. Like the architecture, the mosaics, and the stuccoes, the Palmyrene portraits prove the Hellenization of local art. An obvious fact is conclusive: these are busts, and the Orient did not produce busts. And yet the faces are not those of Greeks or Romans; they are not natural, living, as academic naturalism would say; they exude the "Orient."

On second glance, in fact, one recognizes that indeed those busts can only have come from Palmyra; there is a bizarreness in them that comes from elsewhere, or from a distant past, and which has made these museum pieces highly prized: the faces above all have the blank eyes of a mask, which the sculptor chose for his subjects, and they have what is called frontality in group scenes such as those depicting funerary banquets.

The sculptors inserted in realistic faces eyes that are not those of human beings; they are too large, and their execution is not at all realistic. They are sometimes rounded and globular, as if trying to hypnotize the viewer; sometimes decorative, isolated by deep furrows above and below. They have the lanceolate shape of the leaf of a tree, or the eyelids have an elegantly sinuous outline.

There is a similar shocking expressionism in the frontality of group scenes. Lying on their banquet beds, the figures in scenes of funerary banquets should logically be looking after themselves, their neighbors, and their drinking cups, and this is what they do on Greek funerary bas-reliefs. While borrowing this subject from Greece, the Palmyrene sculptor transformed its spirit: instead of showing us drinkers in action, he interrupted them, made them turn toward us with their cups in their hands, and showed us their faces, lined up like students in a class photo; the animated scene has become a group portrait. This same type of representation is seen later in the Byzantine mosaics of Ravenna, where an entire procession comes to a stop, turns around, and lines up facing the viewer. And so the appearance of this systematic frontality in Palmyrene art appears, rightly or wrongly, to have been a pivotal moment in art history.

The Palmyrene artisans assimilated the details of naturalism, but the spirit of that style escaped them, the life of groups and theatrical illusion remained foreign to them; they hesitated between a symmetrical frontality and the Hellenic recipe, which gave the illusion of naturalness by presenting figures in three-quarters profile, as do our actors, who divide themselves between the partner facing them on stage and the audience in the theater: they must simultaneously perform an action and allow themselves to be seen by the audience.

The art of Palmyra does not exhibit the deep, primary interest in the human body that ancient Greek artists did, nor sensitivity to an incoherence between conventional eyes and the realism of faces. Often the artists simplified details that should have required a meticulous treatment: locks of hair become symmetrically arranged masses, tufts of beards form a forest of small pyramids, and the folds of clothing suggest folds without making us feel the suppleness and the weighty fall of the fabric. Were these simplifications perhaps meant to be decorative? Weren't they rather a naive, artisanal means of putting artistic order into natural confusion? Finally, although the treatment of faces is summary, the jewelry, the hairstyles, and the embroidery of the beautiful clothing are rendered with an epicurean and ostentatious precision.

We can now understand what made these works museum pieces: their style is a hybrid. Local artisans imitated the Greco-Roman art of the portrait, but their hands retained old habits inherited from an Oriental substrata; and to that substrata was added a timeless "primitivism": frontality and the eyes of a mask. This hybrid nature is a sort of originality that minimizes the importance of rather average artistic quality; we see in it a nonacademic freshness.

Palmyrene art had that indigenous sensibility because, in this realm as well, Palmyra came out of the desert too late. It "missed" an initial historical encounter with Hellenism: after Alexander the Great conquered the Orient, Greek art spread as far as India, Pakistan, and Kabul, giving birth to Greco-Mesopotamian, Greco-Iranian, and Greco-Buddhist hybrids. The Palmyrene hybrid was born three centuries later, when the city's annexation to Rome brought it into the great cultural current of the world; Palmyrene art would then have as its model imperial "Roman" art.

Conclusion

Palmyra resembled no other city in the empire. With its art
that was primitivistic, Oriental, a hybrid, or Hellenized; with
its temples with windows and terrace roofs; with its notables who wore Greek or Arab clothing, knowing that Aramaic, Arabic, Greek, or even on great occasions Latin, was
spoken there; we sense that a wind of freedom blew over Palmyra, one of nonconformity, of "multiculturalism." As you will
remember, everything came together in Palmyra: Aram, Arabia, Persia, Syria, Hellenism, the Orient, the West. And yet,
like its neighbor Emesa, it always remained itself, neither Hellenized nor Romanized in its multicultural identity.

Far from ending in universal uniformity, every patchwork
culture, with its diversity, opens the way to inventiveness.

Here is a small, amusing example of this. In July 2015, on
the large frieze of the destroyed Temple of Bel, one could still
see a procession in bas-relief that was coming to adore the
god (figure 10). The men came first, seen in profile, one by
one. But behind them, huddled together, blended together,
as if immobilized by the artist, there was a group of women
wrapped from head to toe in the folds of their veils, a shapeless and surprising mass of vague figures draped and stuck
together, a massing of folds of clothing that scarcely evoked
human shapes: it was a pile of arabesques, more arbitrary than

decorative, and not of folds of clothing carved to depict its weight. . . . We don't understand why they appeared to be immobilized, we don't really know if we were looking at them from the front, in profile, or in three-quarters profile.

It was such an "abstract" design that the viewer didn't know if the figures were walking or had been immobilized by the caprice of an artist who had suddenly broken with the logic of his subject and with realism. Such an image, through its unrealistic stylization, has no equivalent in ancient art that I know of. It caused quite a stir in Malraux's day, and among archeologists of that time: there was no lack of comment about the contemporary audacity of avant-garde painters and the beginnings of abstract art. What is likely, in any case, is that in Palmyra the sculptor, faced with so many possible stylizations inspired by the Orient and the West, decided to have fun by inventing another.

Yes, without a doubt, knowing, wanting to know, only one culture—one's own—is to be condemned to a life of suffocating sameness.

Notes

1. *Palmyre, metropole caravanière* (Paris: Imprimerie nationale, 2001).
2. *L'Empire gréco-romain* (Paris: Le Seuil, coll. "Des travaux," 2005).
3. The rue de Rivoli in Paris bears the name of Napoleon's early victory against the Austrian army at the battle of Rivoli, fought January 14 and 15, 1797. —trans.
4. New excavations, undertaken up to 2011, have taught us more on the Palmyrene home. See Andrew M. Smith II, *Roman Palmyra: Identity, Community, and State Formation* (Oxford, UK: Oxford University Press, 2013), 86–87.
5. The 36,529 French *communes* are significantly smaller than the ninety-six *départements*. —trans.
6. Appian, *The Civil Wars*, V, 9, 37. Translated by John Carter (Penguin Classics, 1996), 283.
7. St. Jerome, *The Life of Malchus, the Captive Monk*, 10. Citation found at http://biblehub.com/library/jerome/the_principal_works_of _st_jerome/the_life_of_malchus_the.htm. —trans.
8. "Khâns ou casernes à Palmyre? A propos des structures visibles sur des photographies aériennes anciennes," *Syria* 71 (1994): 45–112.
9. Saint Jerome, *Life of Malchus*, 4.
10. "Marchands et chefs de caravans à Palmyre," *Syria* 34 (1957): 273.
11. "Tribus et clans dans le Hawran antique," *Syria* 59 (1982).
12. Germaine Tillion, *Le harem et les cousins*, first published in 1966 (Paris: Editions du Seuil, 2015). —trans.
13. Zosimus, *Historia Nova: The Decline of Rome*, I, 39, 1; translated by James J. Buchanan and Harold T. Davis (San Antonio, TX: Trinity University Press, 1967), 24.
14. Javier Teixidor, *Annuaire du Collège de France*, (1996–97): 730–31; Annie and Maurice Sartre, *Zénobie, de Palmyre à Rome* (Paris: Perrin, 2014), 152–53.

15. One should contrast the present version of events with that of Annie and Maurice Sartre, *Zénobie*, 38–187; and with that of Andrew M. Smith II, *Roman Palmyra*, chapter 7.

16. Archeologists have discovered on the ground of the ancient agora ashes of city archives that were discarded and burned, and public seals used on the documents (Henri Seyrig, "Cachets publics des villes de Syrie," *Scripta varia* [Paris: Paul Geuthner, 1998], 427, 435). So this public place in the years that followed Palmyra's demise was left to abandonment and was never cleared. That sacking of the archive warehouse was very calculated: individuals deposited their private contracts, and in particular documents of debt (countless private seals have also been found in the piles of ashes), in the public archives; by destroying the archive warehouse, a paralysis of the social future of the city being punished was assured.

17. *Les Palmyréniens. La Venise des sables* (Paris: Armand Colin, 1992).

18. See the classic book by Aloïs Riegl, *Le Culte moderne des monuments* (Paris: Le Seuil, 1984).

19. "Bêl de Palmyre," *Syria* 48 (1971).